MW00900173

30 Day Keto Meal Plan

Copyright © 2016 by Teresa Mccaine.

All rights reserved.

This document is geared towards providing exact and reliable information in regards to the topic and issue covered. The publication is sold with the idea that the publisher is not required to render accounting, officially permitted, or otherwise, qualified services. If advice is necessary, legal or professional, a practiced individual in the profession should be ordered.

- From a Declaration of Principles which was accepted and approved equally by a Committee of the American Bar Association and a Committee of Publishers and Associations.

In no way is it legal to reproduce, duplicate, or transmit any part of this document, in either electronic means or in printed format. Recording of this publication is strictly prohibited and any storage of this document is not allowed unless with written permission from the publisher. All rights reserved.

The information provided herein is stated to be truthful and consistent, in that any liability, in terms of inattention or otherwise, by any usage or abuse of any policies, processes, or directions contained within is the solitary and utter responsibility of the recipient reader. Under no circumstances will any legal responsibility or blame be held against the publisher for any reparation, damages, or monetary loss due to the information herein, either directly or indirectly.

Respective authors own all copyrights not held by the publisher.

The information herein is offered for informational purposes solely, and is universal as so. The presentation of the information is without contract or any type of guarantee assurance.

The trademarks that are used are without any consent, and the publication of the trademark is without permission or backing by the trademark owner. All trademarks and brands within this book are for clarifying purposes only and are the owned by the owners themselves, not affiliated with this document.

30 DAY KETO MEAL PLAN

ULTIMATE WEIGHT LOSS WITH 120 KETO RECIPES

By

TERESA MCCAINE

Table of Contents

Introduction

The Ketogenic Diet (or the Keto Diet) is one of the most popular diets today. It is spreading quickly among people all over the world, thanks to its many benefits and the fact that it makes life much easier. The Keto Diet, which is based on the premise that the human liver produces ketones, which work as a source of energy, is a low carbohydrate, no sugar diet. When you stop eating recipes that are high in carbohydrates and sugar, your body benefits:

1. Cancer Fighter:

The Keto Diet is all about eating the least amount of carbs as possible and eliminating sugar from all meals! What many people don't realize is that sugar feeds cancer - it empowers it and helps it grow. When you follow the Keto Diet, you will be protecting yourself against cancer and, if you already have cancer, it will help you get rid of it as fast as possible.

2. Weight Loss:

Keto Diet meals are very filling and will help satisfy your hunger with only a small amount of food. This will help get rid of the excess weight – and in a short amount of time!

3. Improve Brain Function:

Eating a lot of sugar will absolutely exhaust your brain and make you feel lazy most of the time. But eating Keto meals will rectify that! Since you will be eating small amounts of carbs, your brain will function much better, helping you to stay motivated and energized throughout the day.

The Keto Diet is not just an ordinary diet that requires you to eat only specific foods; rather, it is a lifestyle that will help improve your stamina, energy and health - while eating absolutely delicious food and keeping your body in its best shape ever!!!

So, no matter if you are a beginner or if you already know your way around the Keto Diet… we have compiled 100 mouthwatering recipes in the form of a meal plan that consists of 25 breakfast recipes, 25 snack recipes, 25 lunch recipes and 25 dinner recipes that are so easy to make! In addition, there are another 20 incredible Keto dessert recipes that will blow your mind - for what is life without dessert?!

In total, you are getting 120 Keto recipes, all of which will help you to make easy changes that will make your life healthier and easier!

Weekly Meal Plan Chart for the Whole Food Diet

Week One Meal Plan

Days	Meals	Recipes	Portion	Nutritional Info
Meal 1	Breakfast	Raspberry Pancakes	1 serving	(Calories: 338 | Total Fat: 10 g | Protein: 31.4 g| Total Carbs: 35.8 g)
	Snack	Zucchini Chips	1 serving	(Calories: 172 | Total Fat: 14.6 g | Protein: 3.9 g| Total Carbs: 10.8 g)
	Lunch	Chicken Breasts with Mushroom Gravy	1 serving	(Calories: 556 | Total Fat: 26.4 g | Protein: 66.2 g| Total Carbs: 10.7 g)
	Snack	Cauliflower Bites	1 serving	(Calories: 131 | Total Fat: 13.2 g | Protein: 1.3 g| Total Carbs: 3.5 g)
	Dinner	Cheese Burger Casserole	1 serving	(Calories: 548 | Total Fat: 36.3 g | Protein: 48.5 g| Total Carbs: 4.4 g)
Meal 2	Breakfast	Hash Bacon Skillet	1 serving	(Calories: 421 | Total Fat: 31.4 g | Protein: 25.4 g| Total Carbs: 8.5 g)
	Snack	Salty Coconut Chips	2 balls	(Calories: 283 | Total Fat: 26.7 g | Protein: 2.7 g| Total Carbs: 12.2 g)
	Lunch	Stuffed Sundried Chicken Tomato	1 serving	(Calories: 283 | Total Fat: 9.8 g | Protein: 37.3 g| Total Carbs: 11.5 g)

	Snack	Almond Brownies	1 serving	(Calories: 142 | Total Fat: 11 g | Protein: 2.9 g| Total Carbs: 9.5 g)
	Dinner	Baked Cheesy Spaghetti	1 serving	(Calories: 711 | Total Fat: 59 g | Protein: 43 g| Total Carbs: 15 g)
Meal 3	Breakfast	Cheesy Onion Quiche	1 serving	(Calories: 374 | Total Fat: 31.7 g | Protein: 18.1 g| Total Carbs: 4.2 g)
	Snack	Peanut Butter Chocolate Smoothie	1 serving	(Calories: 663| Total Fat: 66 g | Protein: 10.5 g| Total Carbs: 20.9 g)
	Lunch	Zucchini Steak Stir Fry	1 serving	(Calories: 306 | Total Fat: 10.9 g | Protein: 45 g| Total Carbs: 5.6 g)
	Snack	Crunchy Pepperoni Chips	1 popsicle	(Calories: 245 | Total Fat: 21.8 g | Protein: 11.2 g| Total Carbs: 0.0 g)
	Dinner	Caramelized Onion with Pork Chops	1 serving	(Calories: 352 | Total Fat: 18.23 g | Protein: 36.98 g| Total Carbs: 6.3 g)
Meal 4	Breakfast	Berry Muffins	2 muffins	(Calories: 368 | Total Fat: 28 g | Protein: 10 g| Total Carbs: 12 g)
	Snack	Roasted Macadamia Nuts	2 balls	(Calories: 641 | Total Fat: 67.7 g | Protein: 7.1 g| Total Carbs: 67.7 g)

	Lunch	Steak Salad	1 serving	(Calories: 384 | Total Fat: 13.8 g | Protein: 46.5 g| Total Carbs: 19.2 g)
	Snack	Bacon Avocado Sticks	1 serving	(Calories: 188 | Total Fat: 17 g | Protein: 4.8 g| Total Carbs: 5.9 g)
	Dinner	Bacon Avocado and Egg Salad	1 serving	(Calories: 569| Total Fat: 247.8 g | Protein: 25.5 g| Total Carbs: 14.7 g)
Meal 5	Breakfast	Spicy Cheddar Muffins	1 serving	(Calories: 200 | Total Fat: 16.5 g | Protein: 11 g| Total Carbs: 3.6 g)
	Snack	Peanut Shake	1 serving	(Calories: 331 | Total Fat: 18 g | Protein: 30.2 g| Total Carbs: 13.4 g)
	Lunch	Parsley Scallops Stew	1 serving	(Calories: 459 | Total Fat: 29.7 g | Protein: 38.9 g| Total Carbs: 8.6 g)
	Snack	Bacon Cauliflower Salad	1 serving	(Calories: 368 | Total Fat: 29.5 g | Protein: 17.7 g| Total Carbs: 11.4 g)
	Dinner	Chocolate Chili	1 serving	(Calories: 493 | Total Fat: 23.9 g | Protein: 11.5 g| Total Carbs: 56.4 g)
Meal 6	Breakfast	Pepperoni Pizza Muffins	1 muffin	(Calories: 238 | Total Fat: 18.8 g | Protein: 15.1 g| Total Carbs: 4 g)

	Snack	Almond Fudge Squares	1 serving	(Calories: 177 | Total Fat: 20.1 g | Protein: 0.4 g| Total Carbs: 0.6 g)
	Lunch	Avocado Chicken Salad	1 serving	(Calories: 570 | Total Fat: 26.6 g | Protein: 68.2 g| Total Carbs: 14.9 g)
	Snack	Onion Bean Stir Fry	1 serving	(Calories: 52 | Total Fat: 1 g | Protein: 2.5 g| Total Carbs: 10.1 g)
	Dinner	Fried Chicken Rice	1 serving	(Calories: 190 | Total Fat: 6.5 g | Protein: 21.1 g| Total Carbs: 13 g)
Meal 7	Breakfast	Nutty Porridge	1 serving	(Calories: 318 | Total Fat: 28 g | Protein: 11.4 g| Total Carbs: 10 g)
	Snack	Roasted Almonds	1 serving	(Calories: 328 | Total Fat: 28.4 g | Protein: 12 g| Total Carbs: 12.2 g)
	Lunch	Pork Chili	1 serving	(Calories: 416 | Total Fat: 16.1 g | Protein: 47.6 g| Total Carbs: 21.9 g)
	Snack	Arugula Strawberry Salad	1 serving	(Calories: 57 | Total Fat: 0.9 g | Protein: 3.2 g| Total Carbs: 11.4 g)
	Dinner	Chicken Curry	1 serving	(Calories: 727| Total Fat: 56.2 g | Protein: 39.9 g| Total Carbs: 18.9 g)

Days	Meals	Recipes	Portion	Nutritional Info
Meal 1	Breakfast	Breakfast Bagels	1 bagel	(Calories: 219 | Total Fat: 17.3 g | Protein: 10.5 g| Total Carbs: 6.9 g)
	Snack	Crunchy Parsnip Chips	1 serving	(Calories: 100 | Total Fat: 0.4 g | Protein: 1.6 g| Total Carbs: 23.9 g)
	Lunch	Lamb Shanks with Tomato Sauce	1 serving	(Calories: 477 | Total Fat: 17.6 g | Protein: 66.8 g| Total Carbs: 10.4 g)
	Snack	Onion Bean Stir Fry	1 serving	(Calories: 52 | Total Fat: 1 g | Protein: 2.5 g| Total Carbs: 10.1 g)
	Dinner	Caramelized Onion Pot Roast	1 serving	(Calories: 716 | Total Fat: 25.3 g | Protein: 106.2 g| Total Carbs: 8.3 g)
Meal 2	Breakfast	Bacon Pancakes	1 serving	(Calories: 541 | Total Fat: 44.8 g | Protein: 13.3 g| Total Carbs: 21.5 g)
	Snack	Strawberry Lemonade	1 serving	(Calories: 65 | Total Fat: 0.3 g | Protein: 1.1 g| Total Carbs: 19.9 g)
	Lunch	Hawaiian Pulled Pork	1 serving	(Calories: 472 | Total Fat: 21.4 g | Protein: 64.8 g| Total Carbs: 0.7 g)

Week Two Meal Plan

	Snack	Bread Sticks	1 serving	(Calories: 247 | Total Fat: 16.1 g | Protein: 7.3 g| Total Carbs: 23 g)
	Dinner	Artichoke Chicken Thighs Skillet	1 serving	(Calories: 540 | Total Fat: 28.5 g | Protein: 60.5 g| Total Carbs: 9.2 g)
Meal 3	Breakfast	Cheesy Scrambled Eggs	1 serving	(Calories: 220 | Total Fat: 16.1 g | Protein: 15.5 g| Total Carbs: 3.5 g)
	Snack	Hemp Vanilla Shake	1 serving	(Calories: 404 | Total Fat: 24.5 g | Protein: 27.7 g| Total Carbs: 21.4 g)
	Lunch	Yellow Chicken Curry	1 serving	(Calories: 507 | Total Fat: 26.8 g | Protein: 58.6 g| Total Carbs: 6.2 g)
	Snack	Zucchini Pizza Bites	1 serving	(Calories: 203 | Total Fat: 15.2 g | Protein: 12 g| Total Carbs: 5.4 g)
	Dinner	Greek Pork Chops	1 serving	(Calories: 373 | Total Fat: 32.7 g | Protein: 18.3 g| Total Carbs: 1.4 g)
Meal 4	Breakfast	Bacon Squash Pancakes	1 serving	(Calories: 503 | Total Fat: 31.4 g | Protein: 32.6 g| Total Carbs: 25.4 g)
	Snack	Keto Guacamole	1 serving	(Calories: 324 | Total Fat: 29.5 g | Protein: 3.4 g| Total Carbs: 17.4 g)

	Lunch	Spaghetti Meatballs	1 serving	(Calories: 723 | Total Fat: 28.6 g | Protein: 77.1 g| Total Carbs: 38.5 g)
	Snack	Cauliflower Pizza	1 serving	(Calories: 78 | Total Fat: 4.2 g | Protein: 6.9 g| Total Carbs: 4.1 g)
	Dinner	Strawberry Chicken Salad	1 serving	(Calories: 735 | Total Fat: 50.5 g | Protein: 54.5 g| Total Carbs: 20.9 g)
Meal 5	Breakfast	Bell Eggs Flowers	1 serving	(Calories: 135 | Total Fat: 8.8 g | Protein: 11.4 g| Total Carbs: 2.9 g)
	Snack	Roasted Pecans	1 cracker	(Calories: 395 | Total Fat: 40.5 g | Protein: 6.1 g| Total Carbs: 8.1 g)
	Lunch	Loaded Beef Minestrone	1 serving	(Calories: 289 | Total Fat: 7.9 g | Protein: 38.6 g| Total Carbs: 16.1 g)
	Snack	Bacon Cauliflower Salad	1 popsicle	(Calories: 368 | Total Fat: 29.5 g | Protein: 17.7 g| Total Carbs: 11.4 g)
	Dinner	Cheesy Garlic Spaghetti	1 serving	(Calories: 587 | Total Fat: 43.6 g | Protein: 19.2 g| Total Carbs: 35.8 g)
Meal 6	Breakfast	Arugula Berry Salad	1 serving	(Calories: 86 | Total Fat: 2.7 g | Protein: 2.8 g| Total Carbs: 15 g)
	Lunch	Rosemary Chicken Stew	1 serving	(Calories: 448 | Total Fat: 19.8 g | Protein: 69.8 g|

				Total Carbs: 19.7 g)
	Snack	Crunchy Parsnip Chips	1 popsicle	(Calories: 100 ǀ Total Fat: 0.4 g ǀ Protein: 1.6 gǀ Total Carbs: 23.9 g)
	Dinner	Honey Chicken Avocado Salad	1 serving	(Calories: 691 ǀ Total Fat: 33 g ǀ Protein: 62.5 gǀ Total Carbs: 37.4 g)
Meal 7	Breakfast	Peanut Butter and Jelly Rolls	1 serving	(Calories: 426 ǀ Total Fat: 34.9 g ǀ Protein: 17.2 gǀ Total Carbs: 14.9 g)
	Snack	Strawberry Lemonade	1 serving	(Calories: 65 ǀ Total Fat: 0.3 g ǀ Protein: 1.1 gǀ Total Carbs: 19.9 g)
	Lunch	Turkey Kale Soup	1 serving	(Calories: 307 ǀ Total Fat: 7.8 g ǀ Protein: 44 gǀ Total Carbs: 13.8 g)
	Snack	Bread Sticks	1 serving	(Calories: 247 ǀ Total Fat: 16.1 g ǀ Protein: 7.3 gǀ Total Carbs: 23 g)
	Dinner	Bell Steak Stir Fry	1 serving	(Calories: 707 ǀ Total Fat: 30.1 g ǀ Protein: 88.9 gǀ Total Carbs: 20.1 g)

Week Three Meal Plan

Days	Meals	Recipes	Portion	Nutritional Info
Meal 1	Breakfast	Pumpkin Doughnuts	1 doughnut	(Calories: 204 | Total Fat: 16.1 g | Protein: 6.3 g| Total Carbs: 10.8 g)
	Snack	Peanut Shake	1 serving	(Calories: 331 | Total Fat: 18 g | Protein: 30.2 g| Total Carbs: 13.4 g)
	Lunch	Chipotle Enchilada Stew	1 serving	(Calories: 578| Total Fat: 19.7 g | Protein: 70.9 g| Total Carbs: 30.6 g)
	Snack	Veggies Chips	1 serving	(Calories: 90 | Total Fat: 0.5 g | Protein: 3 g| Total Carbs: 20.1 g)
	Dinner	Stuffed Bell Peppers	1 serving	(Calories: 673 | Total Fat: 18.1 g | Protein: 55 g| Total Carbs: 17.1 g)
Meal 2	Breakfast	Spinach Muffins	2 muffins	(Calories: 384 | Total Fat: 32 g | Protein: 20 g| Total Carbs: 4 g)
	Snack	Roasted Hazelnuts	1 serving	(Calories: 314 | Total Fat: 30.4 g | Protein: 7.5 g| Total Carbs: 8.3 g)
	Lunch	Pumpkin Oxtail Stew	1 serving	(Calories: 617 | Total Fat: 19.5 g | Protein: 94 g| Total Carbs: 12.4 g)
	Snack	Bacon Cauliflower Salad	1 serving	(Calories: 368	Total Fat: 29.5 g	Protein: 17.7 g|

				Total Carbs: 11.4 g)
	Dinner	Squid Spaghetti	1 serving	(Calories: 317 I Total Fat: 16.5 g I Protein: 24.8 gI Total Carbs: 14 g)
Meal 3	Breakfast	Creamy Egg Salad	1 serving	(Calories: 284I Total Fat: 21.9 g I Protein: 11.7 gI Total Carbs: 11.1 g)
	Snack	Peanut Butter Chocolate Smoothie	1 serving	(Calories: 663I Total Fat: 66 g I Protein: 10.5 gI Total Carbs: 20.9 g)
	Lunch	Sausage Ratatouille Stew	1 serving	(Calories: 616 I Total Fat: 40.8 g I Protein: 22.5 gI Total Carbs: 41 g)
	Snack	Rosemary Crackers	1 serving	(Calories: 272 I Total Fat: 17.1 g I Protein: 17.1 gI Total Carbs: 9.4 g)
	Dinner	Nectarine Grilled Steak	1 serving	(Calories: 612 I Total Fat: 40.1 g I Protein: 51.6 gI Total Carbs: 12.4 g)
Meal 4	Breakfast	Mushroom Spinach Frittata	1 serving	(Calories: 398 I Total Fat: 29 g I Protein: 25 gI Total Carbs: 7 g)
	Snack	Zucchini Chips	1 serving	(Calories: 172 I Total Fat: 14.6 g I Protein: 3.9 gI Total Carbs: 10.8 g)
	Lunch	Garlicky Shrimp	1 serving	(Calories: 683I Total Fat: 50.5 g I Protein: 57.1 gI Total Carbs: 7.1 g)
	Snack	Almond Brownies	1 serving	(Calories: 142 I Total Fat: 11 g I Protein: 2.9 gI Total

				Carbs: 9.5 g)
	Dinner	Garlic Parme-san Salmon Fillets	1 serving	(Calories: 435 | Total Fat: 29 g | Protein: 43.1 g| Total Carbs: 2.4 g)
Meal 5	Breakfast	Hemp Heart Porridge	1 serving	(Calories: 596 | Total Fat: 54.4 g | Protein: 12.5 g| Total Carbs: 22 g)
	Snack	Peanut Shake	1 serving	(Calories: 331 | Total Fat: 18 g | Protein: 30.2 g| Total Carbs: 13.4 g)
	Lunch	Spaghetti Shrimp	1 serving	(Calories: 285 | Total Fat: 7.7 g | Protein: 29.7 g| Total Carbs: 27.5 g)
	Snack	Crunchy Pep-peroni Chips	1 serving	(Calories: 245 | Total Fat: 21.8 g | Protein: 11.2 g| Total Carbs: 0.0 g)
	Dinner	Cauliflower Lasagna	1 serving	(Calories: 239 | Total Fat: 21 g | Protein: 8.4 g| Total Carbs: 5.1 g)
Meal 6	Breakfast	Bell Sausages Casserole	1 serving	(Calories: 348 | Total Fat: 26.4 g | Protein: 22.3 g| Total Carbs: 5 g)
	Snack	Roasted Maca-damia Nuts	1 serving	(Calories: 641 | Total Fat: 67.7 g | Protein: 7.1 g | Total Carbs: 67.7 g)
	Lunch	Chicken Cesar Salad	1 serving	(Calories: 588 | Total Fat: 18.4 g | Protein: 85.6 g| Total Carbs: 23.6 g)
	Snack	Crunchy Pars-nip Chips	1 serving	(Calories: 100	Total Fat: 0.4 g	Protein: 1.6 g| To-

				tal Carbs: 23.9 g)
	Dinner	**Cheesy Nacho Casserole**	1 serviing	(Calories: 459 | Total Fat: 24.8 g | Protein: 9.3 g| Total Carbs: 9.3 g)
Meal 7	Breakfast	**Shakshouka Skillet**	1 serving	(Calories: 123 | Total Fat: 7.2 g | Protein: 7.1 g| Total Carbs: 9 g)
	Snack	**Cauliflower Bites**	1 serving	(Calories: 131 | Total Fat: 13.2 g | Protein: 1.3 g| Total Carbs: 3.5 g)
	Lunch	**Paprika Chicken**	1 serving	(Calories: 643 | Total Fat: 27.5 g | Protein: 89.1 g| Total Carbs: 5.3 g)
	Snack	**Rosemary Crackers**	1 serving	(Calories: 272 | Total Fat: 17.1 g | Protein: 17.1 g| Total Carbs: 9.4 g)
	Dinner	**Creamy Jalapeño Bacon Soup**	1 serving	(Calories: 476 | Total Fat: 63.6 g | Protein: 39.9 g| Total Carbs: 5.4 g)

Week Four Meal Plan

Days	Meals	Recipes	Portion	Nutritional Info
Meal 1	Breakfast	Salmon Frittata	1 serving	(Calories: 100 | Total Fat: 6.1 g | Protein: 11 g| Total Carbs: 0.3 g)
	Snack	Almond Fudge Squares	1 serving	(Calories: 177 | Total Fat: 20.1 g | Protein: 0.4 g| Total Carbs: 0.6 g)
	Lunch	Mediterranean Chicken Salad	1 serving	(Calories: 508 | Total Fat: 17 g | Protein: 57.5 g| Total Carbs: 36.4 g)
	Snack	Arugula Strawberry Salad	1 serving	(Calories: 57 | Total Fat: 0.9 g | Protein: 3.2 g| Total Carbs: 11.4 g)
	Dinner	Orange Beef Stew	1 serving	(Calories: 491 | Total Fat: 25.1 g | Protein: 54.9 g| Total Carbs: 10.9 g)
Meal 2	Breakfast	Cheesy Ham Triangles	1 serving	(Calories: 456 | Total Fat: 45 g | Protein: 39.8 g| Total Carbs: 11.3 g)
	Snack	Peanut Butter Chocolate Smoothie	1 serving	(Calories: 663| Total Fat: 66 g | Protein: 10.5 g| Total Carbs: 20.9 g)
	Lunch	Stuffed Sun-dried Chicken Tomato	1 serving	(Calories: 283 | Total Fat: 9.8 g | Protein: 37.3 g| Total Carbs: 11.5 g)
	Snack	Cauliflower Pizza	1 serving	(Calories: 78	Total Fat: 4.2 g	Protein: 6.9 g| To-

				tal Carbs: 4.1 g)
	Dinner	Shrimp Cauli-flower Curry	1 serving	(Calories: 549| Total Fat: 40.8 g | Protein: 36.6 g| Total Carbs: 16.3 g)
Meal 3	Breakfast	Italian Omelet	1 serving	(Calories: 581 | Total Fat: 49.1 g | Protein: 25.8 g| Total Carbs: 10.5 g)
	Snack	Veggies Chips	1 serving	(Calories: 90 | Total Fat: 0.5 g | Protein: 3 g| Total Carbs: 20.1 g)
	Lunch	Saucy Chicken Drumsticks	1 serving	(Calories: 860 | Total Fat: 30.4 g | Protein: 93.9 g| Total Carbs: 46.8 g)
	Snack	Keto Guacamole	1 serving	(Calories: 324 | Total Fat: 29.5 g | Protein: 3.4 g| Total Carbs: 17.4 g)
	Dinner	Creamy Zucchi-ni Egg Bowl	1 serving	(Calories: 734 | Total Fat: 39.4 g | Protein: 85 g| Total Carbs. 5.8 g)
Meal 4	Breakfast	Spicy Cheddar Muffins	1 serving	(Calories: 200 | Total Fat: 16.5 g | Protein: 11 g| Total Carbs: 3.6 g)
	Snack	Bacon Avocado Sticks	1 serving	(Calories: 188 | Total Fat: 17 g | Protein: 4.8 g| Total Carbs: 5.9 g)
	Lunch	Crust less Pep-peroni Pizza	1 serving	(Calories: 870 | Total Fat: 69.9 g | Protein: 49 g| Total Carbs: 8.5 g)
	Snack	Roasted Pecans	1 serving	(Calories: 395	Total Fat: 40.5 g	Protein: 6.1 g|

				Total Carbs: 8.1 g)
	Dinner	Thai Peanut Chicken	1 serving	(Calories: 430 I Total Fat: 23.2 g I Protein: 49.7 gI Total Carbs: 5.1 g)
Meal 5	Breakfast	Cheesy Onion Quiche	1 serving	(Calories: 374 I Total Fat: 31.7 g I Protein: 18.1 gI Total Carbs: 4.2 g)
	Snack	Zucchini Pizza Bites	1 serving	(Calories: 203 I Total Fat: 15.2 g I Protein: 12 gI Total Carbs: 5.4 g)
	Lunch	Bacon Chicken Sandwich	1 serving	(Calories: 475 I Total Fat: 36.2 g I Protein: 30.1 gI Total Carbs: 7.3 g)
	Snack	Strawberry Lemonade	1 serving	(Calories: 65 I Total Fat: 0.3 g I Protein: 1.1 gI Total Carbs: 19.9 g)
	Dinner	Squid Spaghetti	1 serving	(Calories: 317 I Total Fat: 16.5 g I Protein: 24.8 gI Total Carbs: 14 g)
Meal 6	Breakfast	Peanut Butter and Jelly Rolls	1 serving	(Calories: 426 I Total Fat: 34.9 g I Protein: 17.2 gI Total Carbs: 14.9 g)
	Snack	Salty Coconut Chips	1 serving	(Calories: 283 I Total Fat: 26.7 g I Protein: 2.7 gI Total Carbs: 12.2 g)
	Lunch	Pork Chili	1 serving	(Calories: 416 I Total Fat: 16.1 g I Protein: 47.6 gI Total Carbs: 21.9 g)
	Snack	Arugula Strawberry Salad	1 serving	(Calories: 57 I Total Fat: 0.9 g I Protein: 3.2 gI To-

				tal Carbs: 11.4 g)
	Dinner	Cheesy Garlic Spaghetti	1 serving	(Calories: 587 | Total Fat: 43.6 g | Protein: 19.2 g| Total Carbs: 35.8 g)
Meal 7	Breakfast	Creamy Egg Salad	1 serving	(Calories: 284| Total Fat: 21.9 g | Protein: 11.7 g| Total Carbs: 11.1 g)
	Snack	Roasted Almonds	1 serving	(Calories: 328 | Total Fat: 28.4 g | Protein: 12 g| Total Carbs: 12.2 g)
	Lunch	Loaded Beef Minestrone	1 serving	(Calories: 289 | Total Fat: 7.9 g | Protein: 38.6 g| Total Carbs: 16.1 g)
	Snack	Almond Brownies	1 serving	(Calories: 142 | Total Fat: 11 g | Protein: 2.9 g| Total Carbs: 9.5 g)
	Dinner	Artichoke Chicken Thighs Skillet	1 serving	(Calories: 540 | Total Fat: 28.5 g | Protein: 60.5 g| Total Carbs: 9.2 g)

Breakfast

Raspberry Pancakes

(Prep Time: 20 min | Cooking Time: 10 min | Servings 1)

Ingredients:

- 1 scoop protein powder
- ¾ cup of raspberries
- ½ banana, mashed
- ¼ cup egg whites
- 2 tablespoons Greek yogurt
- 2 tablespoons almond milk
- 1 tablespoon cinnamon
- 1 tablespoon Chia seeds, ground
- Salt

Directions:

1. Mix all the ingredients in a mixing bowl until no lumps are found.

2. Pour half of the batter into a greased pan, cook until the mixture becomes brown on the edges, flip and then cook it on the other side.

3. Repeat the process with the remaining batter and then serve and enjoy.

(Calories: 338 | Total Fat: 10 g | Protein: 31.4 g| Total Carbs: 35.8 g)

Hash Bacon Skillet

(Prep Time: 15 min | Cooking Time: 20 min | Servings 4)

Ingredients:

- 10 bacon strips, diced
- 1 large yellow onion, diced
- 1 large carrot, shredded
- 1 green bell pepper, seeded and diced
- ½ cup Monterrey Jack cheese, shredded
- 1 tablespoon butter
- Black pepper
- Salt

Directions:

1. Cook the bacon in a large skillet until it becomes crispy, then drain it and set it aside.

2. Melt the butter with the remaining bacon fat then add the onion bell pepper and carrots. Cook for 6 to 8 mins, or until softened.

3. Once the time is up, add the cooked bacon, a pinch of salt and pepper, then make 4 small holes for the eggs.

4. Crack each egg in a half and season with some salt and pepper. Cook them until they are done.

5. Serve your bacon skillet warm and enjoy.

(Calories: 421 | Total Fat: 31.4 g | Protein: 25.4 g| Total Carbs: 8.5 g)

Cheesy Onion Quiche

(Prep Time: 15 min | Cooking Time: 34 min | Servings 6)

Ingredients:

- 3 cups Colby Jack cheese, shredded
- 6 eggs
- 1 cup heavy cream
- ½ large white onion, finely chopped
- 1 tablespoon butter
- 1 teaspoon dry thyme
- Black pepper
- Salt

Directions:

1. Preheat the oven to 350 F.

2. Melt the butter in a large skillet. Add the onion for 6 to 8 min until it softens, then set it aside to cool down.

3. Beat the eggs with thyme, heavy cream, a pinch of salt and pepper in a large bowl until they become pale.

4. Lay 2 cups of cheese in the bottom of a greased 10 inch pan, then add the cooked onion followed by the eggs.

5. Sprinkle the remaining cheese on top, then bake for 20 to 25 min.

6. Serve your quiche warm and enjoy.

(Calories: 374 | Total Fat: 31.7 g | Protein: 18.1 g| Total Carbs: 4.2 g)

Berry Muffins

(Prep Time: 15 min | Cooking Time: 25 min | Servings 15)

Ingredients:

- 5 ounces fresh blueberries
- 2 cups almond flour
- 1 cup heavy cream
- 1/8 cup butter
- 2 eggs
- 5 packets Stevia sweetener
- ½ teaspoon baking soda
- ½ teaspoon lemon extract
- Salt

Directions:

1. Preheat the oven to 350 F.

2. Whisk the flour with cream in a large mixing bowl until no lumps are found, then add 1 egg at a time while whisking continuously.

3. Add the lemon extract with baking soda, a pinch of salt, butter and sweetener, then whisk them again.

4. Fold in the blueberries, then pour the batter into a greased muffin pan.

5. Bake for 20 mins until they become golden.

6. Once the time is up, allow the muffins to cool down completely, then serve and enjoy.

(Calories: 184 | Total Fat: 17 g | Protein: 5 g| Total Carbs: 6 g)

Spicy Cheddar Muffins

(Prep Time: 15 min | Cooking Time: 30 min | Servings 9)

Ingredients:

- 2 cups cheddar cheese, shredded
- 1 ¼ cup blanched almond flour
- 3 eggs
- 1 tablespoon of red pepper flakes
- ½ teaspoon of baking soda
- ½ teaspoon of salt

Directions:

1. Preheat the oven to 350 F.

2. Combine the baking soda with flour and salt in a food processor, then pulse them several times while adding one egg at a time until they become well mixed.

3. Add in the remaining ingredients and pulse them again until no lumps are found.

4. Pour the batter into a greased muffin pan and bake them for 25 to 30 mins.

5. Once the time is up, allow to cool for 1 hour. Serve and enjoy.

(Calories: 200 | Total Fat: 16.5 g | Protein: 11 g| Total Carbs: 3.6 g)

Pepperoni Pizza Muffins

(Prep Time: 20 min | Cooking Time: 45 min | Servings 12)

Ingredients:

- 4 eggs
- 1 ½ cup blanched almond flour
- 1 cup cheddar cheese, shredded
- 1 cup Parmesan cheese, grated
- 2/4 cup tomato sauce
- 4 ounces small pepperoni, sliced
- ½ teaspoon baking soda
- Salt

Directions:

1. Preheat the oven to 350 F.

2. Combine the baking soda with flour and a pinch of salt in a food processor, then pulse them several times while adding one egg at a time followed by ¼ cup of the sauce until they become well mixed.

3. Add ½ cup of cheddar with 2 ounces of pepperoni and ½ cup of Parmesan cheese, then pulse again.

4. Pour the batter into a greased muffin pan, then bake for 25 to 30 mins until they are

done.

5. Once the time is up, spread the remaining sauce on the muffins, then top them with the remaining cheese and pepperoni.

6. Bake the muffins for another 15 mins. Serve warm and enjoy.

(Calories: 238 | Total Fat: 18.8 g | Protein: 15.1 g| Total Carbs: 4 g)

Nutty Porridge

(Prep Time: 15 min | Cooking Time: 00 min | Servings 1)

Ingredients:

- 1 cup boiling water
- ¼ cup walnuts
- 2 tablespoons coconut, shredded
- 1 tablespoon Chia seeds
- 1 tablespoon flax seeds
- 1 tablespoon pumpkin seeds
- 1 teaspoon cinnamon
- Salt

Directions:

1. Combine all the ingredients in a food processor or blender and pulse them until they become finely ground.

2. Add the hot water and blend again until smooth.

3. Serve your porridge with your favorite toppings and enjoy.

(Calories: 318 | Total Fat: 28 g | Protein: 11.4 g| Total Carbs: 10 g)

Breakfast Bagels

(Prep Time: 15 min | Cooking Time: 25 min | Servings 6)

Ingredients:

- 1 ½ cup almond flour, blanched
- 5 eggs
- ¼ cup golden flax meal
- 2 tablespoons apple cider vinegar
- 1 tablespoon coconut flour
- 1 teaspoon baking soda
- Salt

Directions:

1. Preheat the oven to 350 F.

2. Combine all the ingredients in a food processor with a pinch of salt and blend them smooth.

3. Pour the batter into 6 greased and dusted donut molds, sprinkle with Chia seeds or sesame seeds and bake them for 20 to 25 mins.

4. Allow the bagels to cool down completely. Serve them and enjoy.

(Calories: 219 | Total Fat: 17.3 g | Protein: 10.5 g| Total Carbs: 6.9 g)

Bacon Pancakes

(Prep Time: 15 min | Cooking Time: 20 min | Servings 4)

Ingredients:

- 1 cup of Carbquick biscuit and baking mix
- 8 bacon strips
- ½ cup heavy cream
- ½ cup butter, unsalted and melted
- ¼ cup water
- 1 tablespoon vanilla syrup
- ½ teaspoon baking soda
- Salt

Directions:

1. Whisk the butter with vanilla syrup and water in a mixing bowl.

2. Mix the Carbquick with baking soda in a mixing bowl then add the butter mix and

whisk them until no lumps are found.

3. Spoon 1/8 of the batter into a greased pan, then top with raw bacon strips.

4. Cook the pancake until the edges start to become brown, then flip and cook it on the other side.

5. Repeat the process with the remaining ingredients. Serve your pancakes and enjoy.

(Calories: 541 | Total Fat: 44.8 g | Protein: 13.3 g| Total Carbs: 21.5 g)

Cheesy Scrambled Eggs

(Prep Time: 10 min | Cooking Time: 10 min | Servings 10)

Ingredients:

- 9 ounces tomato, drained and diced
- 8 ounces ham, diced
- 8 ounces cheddar cheese, shredded
- 4 ounces green onions, sliced
- 10 eggs
- ½ cup heavy cream
- ¼ cup water
- Black pepper
- Salt

Directions:

1. Preheat the oven to 450 F.

2. Whisk the cream with water, eggs, some black pepper and salt in a mixing bowl until they become frothy.

3. Pour the egg mixture on a greased baking sheet and bake for 8 mins, then top with to-

mato, onion, ham and cheese.

4. Bake them for another 2 mins and scramble gently to combine the flavors.

5. Serve your scrambled eggs and enjoy.

(Calories: 220 | Total Fat: 16.1 g | Protein: 15.5 g| Total Carbs: 3.5 g)

Bacon Squash Pancakes

(Prep Time: 10 min | Cooking Time: 12 min | Servings 1)

Ingredients:

- 10 ounces spaghetti squash, cooked and shredded
- 4 bacon strips, cooked and crumbled
- 1 ounce parmesan cheese, grated
- 1 teaspoon onion powder
- 1 teaspoon garlic powder
- Bacon grease
- Black pepper
- Salt

Directions:

1. Melt some bacon grease in a large pan.

2. Mix the remaining ingredients in a mixing bowl, then spoon ½ of the mixture into the greased pan and cook it for 3 to 4 mins on each side or until it done.

3. Repeat the process with the remaining ingredients to make another pancake. Serve and enjoy.

(Calories: 503 | Total Fat: 31.4 g | Protein: 32.6 g| Total Carbs: 25.4 g)

Bell Eggs Flowers

(Prep Time: 10 min | Cooking Time: 4 min | Servings 4)

Ingredients:

- 8 bell pepper slices
- 8 eggs
- Black pepper
- Salt

Directions:

1. Place the bell pepper slices in a greased pan, then surround with eggs.

2. Season them with some salt and pepper. Cook for 3 to 4 mins until they are done.

3. Serve your bell pepper slices and enjoy.

(Calories: 135 | Total Fat: 8.8 g | Protein: 11.4 g| Total Carbs: 2.9 g)

Arugula Berry Salad

(Prep Time: 10 min | Cooking Time: 00 min | Servings 2)

Ingredients:

- 10 ounces baby arugula
- 2 cups blueberries
- ¼ cup avocado oil
- 2 tablespoons fresh orange juice
- 2 tablespoons balsamic vinegar
- 1 tablespoon of Dijon mustard

Directions:

1. Whisk the orange juice with mustard, vinegar and oil in a small bowl to make the dressing.

2. Toss the dressing with arugula and berries in a mixing bowl, then serve it and enjoy.

(Calories: 86 | Total Fat: 2.7 g | Protein: 2.8 g| Total Carbs: 15 g)

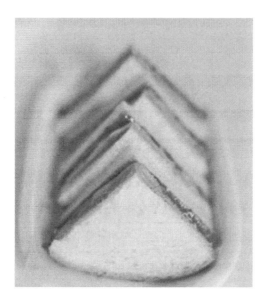

Peanut Butter and Jelly Rolls

(Prep Time: 10 min | Cooking Time: 2 min | Servings 1)

Ingredients:

- 2 eggs
- 3 tablespoons almond flour
- 1 tablespoon butter
- 1 tablespoon coconut flour
- ½ tablespoon jelly
- ½ tablespoon peanut butter
- ½ teaspoon baking powder
- Salt

Directions:

1. Whisk the almond flour with eggs, butter, coconut flour, baking powder and a pinch of salt in a small bowl, then pour the mix into a greased mug to prepare the sandwich.

2. Microwave for 2 mins.

3. Cut the sandwich into 4 slices.

4. Spread the jelly and peanut butter on 2 sandwich slices then cover with the other slices, serve and enjoy.

(Calories: 426 | Total Fat: 34.9 g | Protein: 17.2 g| Total Carbs: 14.9 g)

Pumpkin Doughnuts

(Prep Time: 15 min | Cooking Time: 15 min | Servings 6)

Ingredients:

- 1 cup almond flour
- 3 eggs
- 3 tablespoons butter
- 2 tablespoons erythritol, powdered
- 2 tablespoons pumpkin pie spice
- 1 teaspoon vanilla extract
- ¼ teaspoon baking soda
- ¼ teaspoon cinnamon
- Salt

Directions:

1. Preheat the oven to 350 F.

2. Mix all the ingredients in a mixing bowl until no lumps are found, then spoon the mix into 6 greased donut molds.

3. Bake for 12 to 15 mins, then serve them with your favorite toppings and enjoy.

(Calories: 204 | Total Fat: 16.1 g | Protein: 6.3 g| Total Carbs: 10.8 g)

Spinach Muffins

(Prep Time: 15 min | Cooking Time: 25 min | Servings 24)

Ingredients:

- 16 eggs
- 1 cup cheddar cheese, shredded
- 1 cup heavy cream
- 1 cup frozen spinach, thawed
- 4 teaspoons parsley, finely chopped
- Black pepper
- Salt

Directions:

1. Preheat the oven to 375 F.

2. Mix all the ingredients in a mixing bowl, then spoon them into 24 capacity muffin pan.

3. Bake for 20 to 25 mins.

4. Once the time is up, serve your muffins and enjoy.

(Calories: 192 | Total Fat: 16 g | Protein: 10 g| Total Carbs: 2 g)

Creamy Egg Salad

(Prep Time: 15 min | Cooking Time: 15 min | Servings 4)

Ingredients:

- 8 eggs, boiled and peeled
- 2 white part of green onions, finely chopped
- 2 stalks celery, finely chopped
- 2/3 cup mayonnaise
- 4 lettuce leaves
- 1 teaspoon yellow mustard
- Black pepper
- Salt

Directions:

1. Mix the egg yolks with mustard, mayo and a pinch of salt and pepper in a small bowl until they become creamy.

2. Cut the egg whites into the mixture

3. Stir the egg white dices with mayo mix, onion, celery and a pinch of salt and pepper in a large bowl.

4. Serve your salad with the lettuce leaves and enjoy.

(Calories: 284| Total Fat: 21.9 g | Protein: 11.7 g| Total Carbs: 11.1 g)

Mushroom Spinach Frittata

(Prep Time: 15 min | Cooking Time: 45 min | Servings 6)

Ingredients:

- 10 ounces frozen spinach, thawed
- 8 ounces button mushroom, sliced
- 2 ounces feta cheese
- 4 eggs
- 1 cup milk
- ½ cup mozzarella cheese, shredded
- ¼ cup parmesan cheese, grated
- Black pepper
- Salt

Directions:

1. Preheat the oven to 350 F.
2. Whisk the eggs with milk and a pinch of salt and pepper in a large bowl.
3. Stir in the spinach with mushroom, cheeses and a pinch of salt and pepper.
4. Pour the mix into a greased baking dish, then bake for 45 to 55 min.
5. Serve your frittata warm and enjoy.

(Calories: 143 | Total Fat: 8.5 g | Protein: 12.6 g| Total Carbs: 6 g)

Cheesy Salmon Fritters

(Prep Time: 15 min | Cooking Time: 12 min | Servings 6)

Ingredients:

- 1 pound ricotta cheese
- 6 ounces smoked salmon, finely chopped
- ½ cup parmesan cheese, grated
- 2 eggs
- 6 tablespoons sour cream
- 3 tablespoons olive oil
- 2 tablespoons fresh oregano, finely chopped
- 1 ½ tablespoons coconut flour
- Black pepper
- Salt

Directions:

1. Mix all the ingredients (except for the olive oil) in a mixing bowl until they become like soft dough.

2. Shape the dough into 12 pieces, then press each one of them with your hands to make a small patty.

3. Heat the olive oil in a large pan. Cook, in batches, the salmon patties for 2 to 3 mins on each side.

4. Once the time is up, serve your patties and enjoy.

(Calories: 398 | Total Fat: 29 g | Protein: 25 g| Total Carbs: 7 g)

Hemp Heart Porridge

(Prep Time: 10 min | Cooking Time: 4 min | Servings 2)

Ingredients:

- 1 cup almond milk
- ½ cup hemp hearts, finely chopped
- ¼ cup almond flour
- 2 tablespoons flax seed, ground
- 1 tablespoon Chia seeds
- 5 drops of Stevia, alcohol free
- ¾ teaspoon vanilla extract
- ½ teaspoon cinnamon

Directions:

1. Combine all the ingredients in a small saucepan and bring them to a light boil while stirring continuously.

2. Allow the porridge to cook for 2 mins.

3. Once the time is up, serve it with your favorite toppings and enjoy.

(Calories: 596 | Total Fat: 54.4 g | Protein: 12.5 g| Total Carbs: 22 g)

Bell Sausages Casserole

(Prep Time: 15 min | Cooking Time: 21 min | Servings 4)

Ingredients:

- 10 ounces turkey sausage, crumbled
- 5 eggs
- 1 green bell pepper, finely chopped
- 1 red bell pepper, finely chopped
- ½ cup mozzarella cheese, grated
- Black pepper
- Salt

Directions:

1. Preheat the oven to 450 F.

2. Cook the sausage in a greased skillet for 6 mins, then allow them to cool for 10 mins.

3. Whisk the eggs in a mixing bowl with a pinch of salt and pepper, then add the mozzarella cheese with bell peppers and sausage.

4. Pour the mix into a greased baking dish and bake for 25 min.

5. Once the time is up, serve your sausage casserole and enjoy.

(Calories: 348 | Total Fat: 26.4 g | Protein: 22.3 g| Total Carbs: 5 g)

Shakshouka Skillet

(Prep Time: 15 min | Cooking Time: 40 min | Servings 5)

Ingredients:

- 5 eggs
- 3 plum tomatoes, finely chopped
- 1 white onion, finely chopped
- 1 bell pepper, seeded and finely chopped
- 1 tablespoon ghee
- 2 cloves garlic, minced
- 1 teaspoon paprika
- 1 teaspoon cinnamon
- ¼ teaspoon chili powder
- Black pepper
- Salt

Directions:

1. Melt the ghee in a large pan, add onion and sauté for 10 to 14 mins.

2. Add the bell pepper with garlic and cook for another 10 mins.

3. Stir in the tomato with chili powder, paprika and cinnamon, a pinch of salt and pepper and bring them to a simmer.

4. Crack in the eggs, then season with a pinch of salt and pepper.

5. Cover and cook them for 5 mins.

6. Once the time is up, serve your Shakshouka warm and enjoy.

(Calories: 123 | Total Fat: 7.2 g | Protein: 7.1 g| Total Carbs: 9 g)

Salmon Frittata

(Prep Time: 10 min | Cooking Time: 10 min | Servings 4)

Ingredients:

- 4 ounces salmon, smoked and finely chopped
- 4 eggs
- Black pepper
- Salt

Directions:

1. Preheat the oven broiler.

2. Whisk the eggs in a mixing bowl with a pinch of salt and pepper, then stir in the salmon.

3. Pour the mix into a greased heatproof pan, then bake it until the eggs set.

4. Serve your frittata warm and enjoy.

(Calories: 100 | Total Fat: 6.1 g | Protein: 11 g| Total Carbs: 0.3 g)

Cheesy Ham Triangles

(Prep Time: 20 min | Cooking Time: 20 min | Servings 4)

Ingredients:

- 6 ounce deli ham, sliced
- 4 ounces mozzarella cheese, sliced
- 1 ½ cup Monterrey jack cheese, shredded
- 1 1/3 cup almond flour
- 2 ounces cream cheese
- 1 egg
- 3 tablespoons whey protein powder
- ¼ teaspoon baking soda
- Black pepper
- Salt

Directions:

1. Preheat the oven to 400 F.

2. Combine the cream cheese and Monterrey cheese in a heatproof bowl and microwave them for 2 mins.

3. Beat the egg in a large mixing bowl, then add cream cheese mix with baking soda, al-

mond flour and protein powder.

4. Allow the dough to cool for 5 mins.

5. Place the dough on a greased piece of parchment paper and cover it with another piece of equal size, then roll the dough until it becomes ½ inch thick.

6. Cut the dough into 8 rectangles.

7. Place the slices of mozzarella cheese on half of each rectangle and top with the ham slices.

8. Fold the rectangles, then place them on a lined baking sheet and bake for 20 min.

9. Once the time is up, serve your cheesy pockets and enjoy.

(Calories: 456 | Total Fat: 45 g | Protein: 39.8 g| Total Carbs: 11.3 g)

Italian Omelet

(Prep Time: 10 min | Cooking Time: 4 min | Servings 1)

Ingredients:

- 2 eggs
- 2 ounces cheddar cheese, shredded
- 1 medium tomato, seeded and diced
- ¼ avocado, sliced
- 1 tablespoon butter
- 1 tablespoon water
- Black pepper
- Salt

Directions:

1. Whisk the egg with water and a pinch of salt and pepper in mixing bowl.

2. Melt the butter in a large skillet and add the eggs. Mix, then cook the omelet for 3 mins or until it is done.

3. Lay the cheese on half of the omelet, then top with the avocado and tomato.

4. Fold the omelet, then serve it and enjoy.

(Calories: 581 | Total Fat: 49.1 g | Protein: 25.8 g| Total Carbs: 10.5 g)

Snacks

Zucchini Chips

(Prep Time: 15 min | Cooking Time: 1 h | Servings 1)

Ingredients:

- 1 large zucchini, thinly sliced
- 1 tablespoon olive oil
- Salt

Directions:

1. Preheat the oven to 250 F.

2. Toss the zucchini slices in a large bowl with olive oil and a pinch of salt.

3. Lay the zucchini slices on a lined baking sheet, bake for 30 mins, then flip and bake them for another 30 mins.

4. Once the time is up, serve your chips and enjoy.

(Calories: 172 | Total Fat: 14.6 g | Protein: 3.9 g| Total Carbs: 10.8 g)

Crunchy Parsnip Chips

(Prep Time: 15 min | Cooking Time: 10 min | Servings 2)

Ingredients:

- 2 medium parsnips, peeled and thinly sliced
- Canola oil
- Salt

Directions:

1. Heat to 350 F. canola oil in a large pot.

2. Fry the parsnip chips, in batches, until they become golden brown.

3. Season the parsnip chips with salt, then serve them and enjoy.

(Calories: 100 | Total Fat: 0.4 g | Protein: 1.6 g| Total Carbs: 23.9 g)

Roasted Almonds

(Prep Time: 15 min | Cooking Time: 6 h | Servings 4)

Ingredients:

- ½ pound raw almonds
- ½ tablespoon sea salt

Directions:

1. Place the salt and almonds in a large bowl, cover with filtered water, then let them sit for 8 hrs.

2. Preheat the oven to 170 F or lowest setting.

3. Drain the almonds and season with some sea salt, then spread them on a lined baking sheet.

4. Bake the almonds in the oven for several hours until they become crunchy.

5. Serve your almonds and enjoy.

(Calories: 328 | Total Fat: 28.4 g | Protein: 12 g| Total Carbs: 12.2 g)

Cauliflower Bites

(Prep Time: 15 min | Cooking Time: 50 min | Servings 4)

Ingredients:

- 1 large head cauliflower, cut into florets
- 2 tablespoons ghee
- 2 tablespoons coconut oil
- Salt

Directions:

1. Preheat the oven to 400 F.

2. Mix the butter with coconut oil in a small bowl and microwave until they completely melt.

3. Toss the butter mix with cauliflower florets and some salt then spread it on a lined baking sheet.

4. Bake the cauliflower florets for 40 to 50 mins while stirring every 15 mins.

5. Once the time is up, serve your cauliflower bites and enjoy.

(Calories: 131 | Total Fat: 13.2 g | Protein: 1.3 g| Total Carbs: 3.5 g)

Salty Coconut Chips

(Prep Time: 15 min | Cooking Time: 6 min | Servings 2)

Ingredients:

- 2 cups coconut chips, unsweetened
- Salt

Directions:

1. Place 1 cup of coconut flakes in a heated pan and cook them for 2 to 3 mins or until they become golden brown.

2. Repeat the process with the remaining coconut flakes.

3. Season the coconut flakes with a pinch of salt, then serve and enjoy.

(Calories: 283 | Total Fat: 26.7 g | Protein: 2.7 g| Total Carbs: 12.2 g)

Rosemary Crackers

(Prep Time: 20 min | Cooking Time: 13 min | Servings 4)

Ingredients:

- 1 cup flax seed, ground
- ½ cup parmesan cheese, grated
- 2 eggs
- 1 teaspoon fresh rosemary, minced
- Black pepper
- Salt

Directions:

1. Preheat the oven to 350 F.

2. Mix all the ingredients in a mixing bowl until it becomes dough, then let it sit for 5 mins.

3. Roll the dough on a working surface greased with cooking spray until it becomes thin, then cut into squares.

4. Place the dough squares on lined baking sheet, bake them for 10 mins, then flip them and bake them for another 3 mins.

5. Serve your crackers with some guacamole and enjoy.

(Calories: 272 | Total Fat: 17.1 g | Protein: 17.1 g| Total Carbs: 9.4 g)

Almond Brownies

(Prep Time: 20 min | Cooking Time: 20 min | Servings 20)

Ingredients:

- 5 ounces dark chocolate
- 5 ounces butter, unsalted
- 3 ounces almond flour
- 3 ounces Truvia sweetener
- 4 eggs
- 1 ounce cocoa powder
- ½ teaspoon baking powder
- Salt

Directions:

1. Preheat the oven to 375 F.

2. Combine the chocolate with butter in a small bowl, then melt them in a double boiler.

3. Allow the chocolate mix to cool.

4. Beat the Truvia sweetener with eggs for 3 mins, then add to the chocolate mix while stirring all the time.

5. Mix the baking powder with almond flour, cocoa powder and a pinch of salt in a small bowl, then fold into the chocolate mix until no lumps are found.

6. Pour the batter into a greased tray, then bake for 15 to 20 min.

7. Once the time is up, serve your brownies and enjoy.

(Calories: 142 | Total Fat: 11 g | Protein: 2.9 g| Total Carbs: 9.5 g)

Arugula Strawberry Salad

(Prep Time: 15 min | Cooking Time: 00 min | Servings 2)

Ingredients:

- 6 ounces baby arugula
- 2/3 cups strawberries, sliced
- 2/3 cups blackberries

Directions:

1. Toss all the ingredients in a large bowl then serve them and enjoy.

(Calories: 57 | Total Fat: 0.9 g | Protein: 3.2 g| Total Carbs: 11.4 g)

Almond Fudge Squares

(Prep Time: 15 min | Cooking Time: 00 min | Servings 12)

Ingredients:

- 1 cup coconut oil
- 1 cup almond butter
- ¼ cup coconut milk
- 1 teaspoon vanilla extract
- Stevia

Directions:

1. Combine the coconut oil with peanut butter in a small bowl and microwave them until they melt.

2. Transfer the melted coconut and peanut butter into a blender with the vanilla, coconut milk and a few drops of Stevia to your taste, then blend them smooth.

3. Pour the batter into a greased baking dish and refrigerate it for 3 hours until it hardens.

4. Once the time is up, serve your fudge and enjoy.

(Calories: 177 | Total Fat: 20.1 g | Protein: 0.4 g| Total Carbs: 0.6 g)

Onion Bean Stir Fry

(Prep Time: 15 min | Cooking Time: 30 min | Servings 4)

Ingredients:

- 1 pound green beans, trimmed
- ½ white onion, thinly sliced
- ½ cup water
- 2 tablespoons avocado oil
- 1 tablespoon coconut aminos
- Black pepper
- Salt

Directions:

1. Heat the avocado oil in a large pot and sauté onions for 6 mins.

2. Add in the remaining ingredients and cook them with the lid on for 15 mins until the beans become tender.

3. Once the time is up, remove the lid and cook the beans until no liquid is left.

4. Serve your stir fry and enjoy.

(Calories: 52 | Total Fat: 1 g | Protein: 2.5 g| Total Carbs: 10.1 g)

Bacon Cauliflower Salad

(Prep Time: 15 min | Cooking Time: 16 min | Servings 2)

Ingredients:

- 1 pound broccoli florets
- 1 cup coconut cream
- 10 bacon strips, cooked and crumbled

Directions:

1. Bring a salted pot of water to a boil and blanch in the broccoli for 3 mins.

2. Toss the bacon with cream, cauliflower and a pinch of salt in a mixing bowl then serve them and enjoy.

(Calories: 368 | Total Fat: 29.5 g | Protein: 17.7 g| Total Carbs: 11.4 g)

Peanut Butter Chocolate Smoothie

(Prep Time: 15 min | Cooking Time: 00 min | Servings 1)

Ingredients:

- 1 cup coconut milk, unsweetened
- 1 tablespoon peanut butter powder, unsweetened
- 1 tablespoon cocoa powder, unsweetened
- 5 drops Stevia

Directions:

1. Combine all the ingredients in a blender and blend until smooth.
2. Serve your smoothie and enjoy.

(Calories: 663| Total Fat: 66 g | Protein: 10.5 g| Total Carbs: 20.9 g)

Strawberry Lemonade

(Prep Time: 10 min | Cooking Time: 00 min | Servings 6)

Ingredients:

- 1 pint strawberries, sliced
- 8 cups water
- 2 cups ice cubes
- The juice of 6 lemons
- ½ teaspoon Stevia

Directions:

1. Combine all the ingredients in a large jug and stir them.
2. Serve your lemonade and enjoy.

(Calories: 65 | Total Fat: 0.3 g | Protein: 1.1 g| Total Carbs: 19.9 g)

Hemp Vanilla Shake

(Prep Time: 10 min | Cooking Time: 00 min | Servings 1)

Ingredients:

- 2 ounces kale leaves
- 1 cup ice cubes, crushed
- 1/3 cup water
- 1 scoop whey protein powder
- 2 tablespoons hemp seeds
- 1 tablespoon chocolate chips
- 1 tablespoon coconut oil
- 10 drops of vanilla Stevia
- ¼ teaspoon peppermint extract

Directions:

1. Combine all the ingredients in a blender and blend them smooth.
2. Serve your shake and enjoy.

(Calories: 404 | Total Fat: 24.5 g | Protein: 27.7 g| Total Carbs: 21.4 g)

Peanut Shake

(Prep Time: 10 min | Cooking Time: 00 min | Servings 1)

Ingredients:

- 1 cup ice cubes
- ½ cup water
- 1 scoop protein powder
- 2 tablespoons peanut butter
- 1 teaspoon vanilla extract
- 10 drops of Stevia

Directions:

1. Combine all the ingredients in a blender and blend them smooth.
2. Serve your shake and enjoy.

(Calories: 331 | Total Fat: 18 g | Protein: 30.2 g| Total Carbs: 13.4 g)

Crunchy Pepperoni Chips

(Prep Time: 10 min | Cooking Time: 1min | Servings 2)

Ingredients:

- 18 pepperoni slices

Directions:

1. Lay 2 towels on a baking sheet, cover with pepperoni slices then cover with another towel.

2. Microwave the pepperoni slices until they become crispy

3. Serve your chips and enjoy.

(Calories: 245 | Total Fat: 21.8 g | Protein: 11.2 g| Total Carbs: 0.0 g)

Bread Sticks

(Prep Time: 15 min | Cooking Time: 20 min | Servings 5)

Ingredients:

- 1 cup almond flour
- 1 cup warm water
- ¾ cup flax meal
- ¼ cup coconut flour
- 2 tablespoons Chia seeds, ground
- 2 tablespoons psyllium husk
- Black pepper
- Salt

Directions:

1. Combine all the ingredients in a mixing bowl and knead them slightly until you get soft dough, then let it rest for 20 mins in the fridge.

2. Preheat the oven to 350 F.

3. Divide the dough into 4 pieces and divide each piece into 5 balls.

4. Roll the dough balls after wetting your hands with some water, then roll them gently to

make breadsticks.

5. Place the sticks in a lined baking sheet, brush them with some egg yolk then season them with some salt and pepper.

6. Bake the breadsticks for 15 to 20 min,s then serve them and enjoy.

(Calories: 247 | Total Fat: 16.1 g | Protein: 7.3 g| Total Carbs: 23 g)

Zucchini Pizza Bites

(Prep Time: 15 min | Cooking Time: 8 min | Servings 2)

Ingredients:

- 1 zucchini, trimmed and thickly sliced
- 1 cup mozzarella cheese, shredded
- ¼ cup spaghetti sauce
- Pepperoni slices
- Black pepper
- Salt

Directions:

1. Preheat the oven to 350 F.

2. Season the zucchini slices with some salt and pepper, then spread sauce on top followed by the mozzarella cheese and some pepperoni slices.

3. Bake the zucchini pizzas for 5 to 8 mins or until the cheese melts then serve them and enjoy.

(Calories: 203 | Total Fat: 15.2 g | Protein: 12 g| Total Carbs: 5.4 g)

Cauliflower Pizza

(Prep Time: 15 min | Cooking Time: 30 min | Servings 8)

Ingredients:

- 4 cups cauliflower rice
- 3 cups mozzarella cheese
- 4 eggs
- 3 teaspoons dry oregano
- 4 cloves garlic, minced
- Black pepper
- Salt

Directions:

1. Preheat the oven to 425 F.

2. Microwave the cauliflower rice for 10 mins.

3. Once the time is up, add the eggs with oregano, garlic, 2 cups of cheese, a pinch of salt and pepper, then mix them with a fork.

4. Divide the mix in half and place each on a baking sheet, then shape them into a pizza crust.

5. Bake the crust for 25 mins.

6. Once the time is up, sprinkle the remaining cup of cheese on the crusts, then bake them for another 5 mins.

7. Serve your pizzas and enjoy.

(Calories: 78 | Total Fat: 4.2 g | Protein: 6.9 g| Total Carbs: 4.1 g)

Veggies Chips

(Prep Time: 15 min | Cooking Time: 10 min | Servings 10)

Ingredients:

- 2 carrots, thinly sliced
- 1 large sweet potato, thinly sliced
- 2 celeriac, thinly sliced
- 3 beets, thinly sliced
- Avocado oil
- Salt

Directions:

1. Heat 2 inches of avocado oil in a large pan, then fry the veggies chips in batches, then drain them and set them aside.

2. Toss the chips with some salt then serve them and enjoy.

(Calories: 90 | Total Fat: 0.5 g | Protein: 3 g| Total Carbs: 20.1 g)

Keto Guacamole

(Prep Time: 15 min | Cooking Time: 16 min | Servings 4)

Ingredients:

- 3 ripe avocados, peeled
- 1 bunch cilantro leaves
- ½ white onion, finely chopped
- The juice of 2 limes
- 2 cloves of garlic, minced
- ½ teaspoon paprika
- Black pepper
- Salt

Directions:

1. Combine all the ingredients in a food processor with a pinch of salt and pepper, then blend smooth.

2. Adjust the seasoning of the guacamole and enjoy.

(Calories: 324 | Total Fat: 29.5 g | Protein: 3.4 g| Total Carbs: 17.4 g)

Bacon Avocado Sticks

(Prep Time: 15 min | Cooking Time: 15 min | Servings 2)

Ingredients:

- 6 avocado slices

- 3 bacon slices, cut in half

- Black pepper

- Salt

Directions:

1. Preheat the oven to 425 F.

2. Wrap each slice of bacon around an avocado slice, then place them on a lined baking sheet.

3. Bake the avocado slices for 12 to 15 mins, then serve them and enjoy.

(Calories: 188 | Total Fat: 17 g | Protein: 4.8 g| Total Carbs: 5.9 g)

Roasted Macadamia Nuts

(Prep Time: 15 min | Cooking Time: 7 h | Servings 6)

Ingredients:

- 4 cups macadamia nuts
- ½ tablespoon sea salt

Directions:

1. Place the salt and macadamias in a large bowl, cover with filtered water, then let them sit for 8 hours.

2. Preheat the oven to 170 F or the lowest setting.

3. Drain the macadamia nuts, season them with some sea salt, then spread them on a lined baking sheet.

4. Bake the macadamia nuts in the oven for several hours until they become crunchy.

5. Serve your macadamias and enjoy.

(Calories: 641 | Total Fat: 67.7 g | Protein: 7.1 g| Total Carbs: 67.7 g)

Roasted Hazelnuts

(Prep Time: 15 min | Cooking Time: 7 h | Servings 6)

Ingredients:

- 4 cups hazelnuts
- ½ tablespoon sea salt

Directions:

1. Place the salt and hazelnuts in a large bowl, cover with filtered water, then let them sit for 8 hours.

2. Preheat the oven to 170 F or its lowest setting.

3. Drain the hazelnuts, season them with sea salt, then spread them on a lined baking sheet.

4. Bake the hazelnuts in the oven for several hours until they become crunchy.

5. Serve your hazelnuts and enjoy.

(Calories: 314 | Total Fat: 30.4 g | Protein: 7.5 g| Total Carbs: 8.3 g)

Roasted Pecans

(Prep Time: 15 min | Cooking Time: 7 h | Servings 4)

Ingredients:

- 4 cups pecans
- ½ tablespoon sea salt

Directions:

1. Place the salt and pecans in a large bowl, cover them with filtered water, then let them sit for 8 hours.

2. Preheat the oven to 170 F or its lowest setting.

3. Drain the pecans, season them with some sea salt, then spread them on a lined baking sheet.

4. Bake the pecans in the oven for several hours until they become crunchy.

5. Serve your pecans and enjoy.

(Calories: 395 | Total Fat: 40.5 g | Protein: 6.1 g| Total Carbs: 8.1 g)

Lunch

Chicken Breasts with Mushroom Gravy

(Prep Time: 20 min | Cooking Time: 6 h 8 min | Servings 4)

Ingredients:

- 4 chicken breasts
- 4 cups chicken broth
- 2 cups mushroom, sliced
- ¼ cup chickpea flour
- 2 tablespoons butter
- 1 tablespoon coconut oil
- 1 tablespoon fresh tarragon, finely chopped
- 1 teaspoon mustard
- ½ teaspoon onion powder
- ½ teaspoon garlic powder
- Black pepper
- Salt

Directions:

1. Melt the butter in a large skillet, add mushrooms and sauté for 4 mins.

2. Season the chicken breasts with some salt and pepper, then toss them in a zip lock bag with the chickpea flour.

3. Melt the coconut oil in a large skillet and add chicken breasts; brown for 2 mins on each side.

4. Stir the chicken breasts with the cooked mushrooms and the remaining ingredients in a slow cooker.

5. Cook for 6 hours on low.

6. Once the time is up, adjust the seasoning of the stew then serve it warm and enjoy.

(Calories: 556 | Total Fat: 26.4 g | Protein: 66.2 g| Total Carbs: 10.7 g)

Stuffed Sundried Chicken Tomato

(Prep Time: 20 min | Cooking Time: 6 h 10 min | Servings 2)

Ingredients:

- •2 chicken breasts, butterflied
- •1 cup oily sundried tomato
- •½ cup oily sundried tomato, finely chopped
- •½ cup mozzarella cheese, shredded
- •½ cup chicken broth
- •1 teaspoon tahini sauce
- •Black pepper
- •Salt

Directions:

1. Season the chicken breasts with some salt and pepper, then coat with the tahini sauce.

2. Mix the chopped tomato with cheese in a small bowl to make the filling, then place it on the chicken breasts.

3. Wrap the breasts and secure them with some toothpicks.

4. Heat the oil in a large skillet and brown the chicken breasts for 3 to 5 mins on each side.

5. Stir the broth with whole sundried tomato in a slow cooker then add the chicken.

6. Cook the chicken for 6 hours on low.

7. Once the time is up, serve your stuffed chicken breasts warm and enjoy.

(Calories: 283 | Total Fat: 9.8 g | Protein: 37.3 g| Total Carbs: 11.5 g)

Zucchini Steak Stir Fry

(Prep Time: 15 min | Cooking Time: 14 min | Servings 2)

Ingredients:

- 10 ounces beef steak, thinly sliced
- 1 large zucchini, quartered and sliced
- 1 bunch fresh spinach
- 2 tablespoons tamari sauce
- 2 tablespoons avocado oil
- 2 cloves garlic
- Black pepper
- Salt

Directions:

1. Heat the oil in a large pan and sauté beef for 5 mins.

2. Add the zucchini and cook for another 5 mins, while stirring often.

3. Stir in the garlic with spinach, tamari sauce, a pinch of salt and pepper, then cook for 3 to 4 mins.

4. Serve your stirfry and enjoy.

(Calories: 306 | Total Fat: 10.9 g | Protein: 45 g| Total Carbs: 5.6 g)

Steak Salad

(Prep Time: 15 min | Cooking Time: 12 min | Servings 2)

Ingredients:

- ½ pound steak
- 2 handfuls green leaves
- 2 plum tomatos, seeded and diced
- ¼ cup tamari sauce
- 1 tablespoon olive oil
- 1 tablespoon avocado oil
- ½ tablespoon fresh lemon juice
- Black pepper
- Salt

Directions:

1. Season the steak with some salt and pepper, then add the tamari sauce and refrigerate for 30 mins.

2. Heat the avocado oil in a large pan, add steak and cook for 5 to 6 mins on each side

then slice.

3. Whisk the olive oil with lemon juice in a small bowl to make the dressing.

4. Toss the green leaves with tomato and the dressing in a large serving bowl, then top with the sliced steak.

5. Serve your steak salad and enjoy.

(Calories: 384 | Total Fat: 13.8 g | Protein: 46.5 g| Total Carbs: 19.2 g)

Parsley Scallops Stew

(Prep Time: 10 min | Cooking Time: 5 min | Servings 2)

Ingredients:

- 1 pound large scallops
- ¼ cup Italian parsley, finely chopped
- ¼ cup ghee
- 1 green onion, sliced
- 1 teaspoon fresh lemon zest, grated
- 1 teaspoon olive oil
- 4 cloves of garlic, minced
- 1/8 teaspoon paprika
- Black pepper
- Salt

Directions:

1. Season the scallops with some salt and pepper, then toss with the olive oil and paprika.

2. Coat a skillet with some ghee, then sauté the scallops for 2 mins on each side.

3. Stir the ghee with garlic and cook for 30 secs.

4. Combine the lemon zest with green onion and parsley.

5. Adjust the seasoning of the stew then serve it warm and enjoy.

(Calories: 459 | Total Fat: 29.7 g | Protein: 38.9 g| Total Carbs: 8.6 g)

Avocado Chicken Salad

(Prep Time: 10 min | Cooking Time: 00 min | Servings 2)

Ingredients:

- 1 pound chicken, cooked and shredded
- 2 ripe avocados, diced
- 1 plum tomato, seeded and diced
- ¼ cup white onion, diced
- 4 tablespoons fresh lime juice
- Black pepper
- Salt

Directions:

1. Toss all the ingredients in a large bowl with a pinch of salt and pepper.
2. Serve your salad and enjoy.

(Calories: 570 | Total Fat: 26.6 g | Protein: 68.2 g| Total Carbs: 14.9 g)

Pork Chili

(Prep Time: 15 min | Cooking Time: 10 h | Servings 6 to 8)

Ingredients:

- 2 pounds pork roast, trimmed
- 28 ounces canned fire roasted tomato
- 14 ounces canned tomato sauce
- 2 yellow onions, finely chopped
- 1 yellow bell pepper, seeded and diced
- 1 red bell pepper, seeded and diced
- 1/3 cup hot sauce
- 3 tablespoons paprika
- 2 tablespoons garlic powder
- 2 tablespoons chili powder
- 1 tablespoon cumin
- ½ tablespoon red pepper flakes
- 2 teaspoons cayenne pepper
- 1 clove garlic, minced

• Black pepper

• Salt

Directions:

1. Season the pork roast with some salt and pepper, then place it in a crockpot and add the remaining ingredients.

2. Cook for 8 to 10 hours on low.

3. Drain and shred the roast and stir back into the pot.

4. Adjust the seasoning of the stew then serve it warm and enjoy.

(Calories: 416 | Total Fat: 16.1 g | Protein: 47.6 g| Total Carbs: 21.9 g)

Lamb Shanks with Tomato Sauce

(Prep Time: 20 min | Cooking Time: 4 h 25 | Servings 6)

Ingredients:

- 3 pounds lamb shanks
- 14 ounces tomato, finely chopped
- 3 carrots, finely chopped
- 1 large yellow onion, diced
- 3 cups mushroom, finely chopped
- ¾ cup chicken broth
- 1 tablespoon avocado oil
- 2 tablespoons fresh basil, finely chopped
- 2 tablespoons thyme leaves
- 2 tablespoons fresh lemon juice
- 1 tablespoon fresh oregano, finely chopped
- 3 cloves garlic, minced
- Black pepper
- Salt

Directions:

1. Heat half of the avocado oil in a large skillet and brown half of the lamb shanks for 5 mins, then set them aside.

2. Repeat the process with the remaining oil and lamb shanks, then set them aside as well.

3. Cook the carrots with onion and garlic in the same skillet for 5 mins.

4. Transfer the onion mix to a slow cooker, then add the lamb shanks and top them with the remaining ingredients.

5. Cook them for 4 hours on high.

6. Drain the shanks, set them aside then blend the remaining ingredients in the pot with an Immersion blender or food processor until they become smooth to make the sauce.

7. Serve your lamb shanks warm with the sauce and enjoy.

(Calories: 477 | Total Fat: 17.6 g | Protein: 66.8 g| Total Carbs: 10.4 g)

Hawaiian Pulled Pork

(Prep Time: 15 min | Cooking Time: 10 h | Servings 6)

Ingredients:

- 3 pounds pork roast
- 2 tablespoons liquid smoke
- 4 cloves garlic
- Black pepper
- Salt
- Bacon

Directions:

1. Lay the bacon strips in the bottom of a slow cooker.
2. Make 4 small slits in the pork roast and place a clove of garlic in each slit.
3. Season the roast with some salt and pepper and add bacon strips.
4. Cook the roast for 4 to 5 hours on high, or 8 to 10 hours on low.
5. Pull apart the roast with a fork then serve it warm and enjoy.

(Calories: 472 | Total Fat: 21.4 g | Protein: 64.8 g| Total Carbs: 0.7 g)

Yellow Chicken Curry

(Prep Time: 15 min | Cooking Time: 7 h 5 min | Servings 4)

Ingredients:

- 2 ½ pound chicken breasts, diced
- 3 cups chicken broth
- 1 cup coconut milk
- 1 cup yellow onion, finely chopped
- 2 tablespoons yellow curry powder
- 1 tablespoon coconut oil
- 2 cloves garlic, minced
- 1 teaspoon fresh ginger, minced
- Black pepper
- Salt

Directions:

1. Heat the oil in a large skillet and sauté the onion for 3 mins, then add the garlic and cook them for 1 min.

2. Transfer the onion with the remaining ingredients, except for the milk, into a slow cooker.

3. Cook the stew for 3 hours on high or 6 hours on low.

4. Stir in the coconut milk and cook the stew for 1 hour on low.

5. Adjust the seasoning of the stew then serve it warm and enjoy.

(Calories: 507 | Total Fat: 26.8 g | Protein: 58.6 g| Total Carbs: 6.2 g)

Spaghetti Meatballs

(Prep Time: 20 min | Cooking Time: 7 h 45 min | Servings 6)

Ingredients:

- 3 pounds spaghetti squash, halved and seeded
- 2 pounds lean beef, minced
- 1 pound lean pork, minced
- 4 eggs
- 3 cups marinara sauce
- 1 yellow onion, diced
- ½ cup almond flour
- 2 tablespoons dry oregano
- 1 tablespoon fresh basil, finely chopped
- 1 tablespoon garlic powder
- 1/8 teaspoon cayenne pepper
- Black pepper
- Salt

Directions:

1. Preheat the oven to 375 F.

2. Mix the pork and beef with eggs, onion, oregano, garlic, cayenne pepper, flour, a pinch of salt and pepper in a large mixing bowl then shape into small meatballs.

3. Mix the basil with marinara sauce in a bowl.

4. Place the meatballs in a greased crockpot and pour the marinara sauce all over them, then cook them for 7 hours on low.

5. Place the spaghetti squash, halved, on a lined baking sheet and bake for 35 to 45 mins.

6. Scrape the flesh of the squash with a fork, then serve it with the marinara meatballs and enjoy.

(Calories: 723 | Total Fat: 28.6 g | Protein: 77.1 g| Total Carbs: 38.5 g)

Loaded Beef Minestrone

(Prep Time: 20 min | Cooking Time: 6 h 6 min | Servings 4)

Ingredients:

- 1 pound lean beef, minced
- 28 ounces canned diced tomato
- 3 cups water, boiling
- 2 zucchinis, diced
- 1 carrot, diced
- 1 stalk celery, diced
- 1 medium yellow onion, diced
- ½ cup vegetable broth
- 1 tablespoon garlic, minced
- ½ teaspoon dry basil
- ½ teaspoon dry oregano
- Black pepper
- Salt

Directions:

1. Brown the beef in a large skillet for 4 to 6 mins.

2. Transfer the beef into a large crockpot with the remaining ingredients.

3. Cook for 5 to 6 hours on low.

4. Adjust the seasoning of the stew then serve it warm and enjoy.

(Calories: 289 | Total Fat: 7.9 g | Protein: 38.6 g| Total Carbs: 16.1 g)

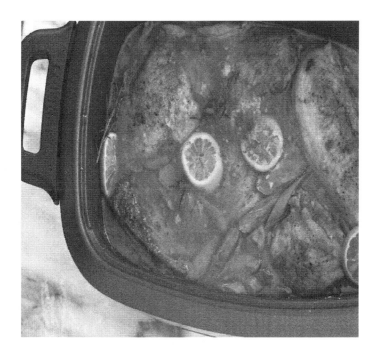

Rosemary Chicken Stew

(Prep Time: 20 min | Cooking Time: 6 h 20 min | Servings 8)

Ingredients:

- 4 pounds chicken thighs, boneless
- 8 carrots, sliced
- 3 yellow onions, thinly sliced
- ¾ cup chicken broth
- ½ cup fresh lemon juice
- ½ cup chickpea flour
- 1 fresh lemon, thinly sliced
- 1 tablespoon olive oil
- 4 cloves garlic, finely chopped
- 3 rosemary sprigs
- Black pepper
- Salt

Directions:

1. Season the chicken with some salt and pepper, then toss it in a large zip lock bag with

the chickpea flour.

2. Heat the oil in a large pot and brown chicken for 3 mins on each side, then drain it and set it aside.

3. Sauté the garlic with onion in the same skillet for 8 mins, then transfer it into a slow cooker with the brown chicken and the remaining ingredients.

4. Cook for 6 hours on low.

5. Once the time is up, serve your stew warm and enjoy.

(Calories: 448 | Total Fat: 19.8 g | Protein: 69.8 g| Total Carbs: 19.7 g)

Turkey Kale Soup

(Prep Time: 15 min | Cooking Time: 40 min | Servings 3)

Ingredients:

- 3 cups turkey meat, roughly chopped
- 4 cups chicken stock
- 3 carrots, sliced
- 2 cups kale
- ½ yellow onion, finely chopped
- ½ tablespoon bacon grease
- ½ teaspoon dry rosemary
- 1 clove garlic, minced
- Black pepper
- Salt

Directions:

1. Melt the bacon grease in a large pot and sauté the onion for 4 mins, then add the carrots with garlic and cook for 3 mins.

2. Stir in the rosemary with stock and bring them to a boil, then simmer them for 20 mins on low heat.

3. Add the turkey with kale, then simmer the soup for 5 min.

4. Adjust the seasoning of the soup then serve it warm and enjoy.

(Calories: 307 | Total Fat: 7.8 g | Protein: 44 g| Total Carbs: 13.8 g)

Chipotle Enchilada Stew

(Prep Time: 15 min | Cooking Time: 8 h | Servings 4)

Ingredients:

- 2 pounds chicken breasts
- 14 ounces tomato, diced
- 1 white onion, finely chopped
- 1 green bell pepper, finely chopped
- 4 ounces canned chili peppers
- 3 jalapenos, finely chopped
- 2 cups chicken stock
- 1 tablespoon chipotle seasoning
- 1 tablespoon chili powder
- 1 tablespoon cumin
- Black pepper
- Salt

Directions:

1. Season the chicken with salt and pepper, then rub it with the chipotle seasoning.

2. Place the chicken breasts in a slow cooker with the remaining ingredients, then cook for 5 hours on low.

3. Drain and shred the chicken and stir it back into the pot.

4. Adjust the seasoning of the stew then serve it warm and enjoy.

(Calories: 578| Total Fat: 19.7 g | Protein: 70.9 g| Total Carbs: 30.6 g)

Pumpkin Oxtail Stew

(Prep Time: 15 min | Cooking Time: 10 h | Servings 6)

Ingredients:

- 4 pounds oxtail cut into pieces
- 6 cups water
- 4 cups canned tomato, diced
- 2 cups pumpkin, diced
- 2 cloves garlic, minced
- 4 teaspoons paprika
- Black pepper
- Salt

Directions:

1. Season the oxtail pieces with salt and pepper, then stir into a large pot with the remaining ingredients.

2. Cook for 10 hours.

3. Adjust the seasoning of the stew, then serve it warm and enjoy.

(Calories: 617 | Total Fat: 19.5 g | Protein: 94 g| Total Carbs: 12.4 g)

Sausage Ratatouille Stew

(Prep Time: 15 min | Cooking Time: 16 min | Servings 4)

Ingredients:

- 1 pound Italian sausage, crumbled
- 1 pound zucchini, halved and sliced
- 25 ounces pasta sauce
- 1 large eggplant, diced
- 1 green bell pepper, sliced
- 1 yellow onion, quartered and thinly sliced
- 2 cloves garlic, crushed
- Black pepper
- Salt

Directions:

1. Stir all the ingredients in a large slow cooker, then season with salt and pepper.
2. Cook for 4 hours on high.
3. Once the time is up, serve your stew warm and enjoy.

(Calories: 616 | Total Fat: 40.8 g | Protein: 22.5 g| Total Carbs: 41 g)

Garlicky Shrimp

(Prep Time: 15 min | Cooking Time: 50 min | Servings 2 to 3)

Ingredients:

- 2 pounds large shrimp
- ¾ cup olive oil
- 1 teaspoon paprika
- 4 cloves garlic, thinly sliced
- Black pepper
- Salt

Directions:

1. Combine the paprika with olive oil and garlic in a slow cooker, then cook 30 mins on high.

2. Season the shrimp with salt and pepper, then stir it into the pot and cook it for 10 mins on high pressure.

3. Serve your garlicky shrimp warm with some rice and enjoy

(Calories: 683| Total Fat: 50.5 g | Protein: 57.1 g| Total Carbs: 7.1 g)

Spaghetti Shrimp

(Prep Time: 15 min | Cooking Time: 20 min | Servings 2)

Ingredients:

- 2 to 3 pounds spaghetti squash, halved and seeded
- ¾ pound large shrimp
- 32 ounces chicken broth
- 1 yellow onion, finely chopped
- 1 tablespoon ghee
- Black pepper
- Salt

Directions:

1. Stir the onion, broth and ghee into a slow cooker, then add the squash with the open side facing down.

2. Add the shrimp, then season with some salt and pepper.

3. Cook for 20 mins on high.

4. Drain the squash halves and allow them to cool slightly, then scrape out the flesh with a fork.

5. Stir the spaghetti into the pot with the shrimp and broth then serve it warm and enjoy.

(Calories: 285 | Total Fat: 7.7 g | Protein: 29.7 g| Total Carbs: 27.5 g)

Chicken Cesar Salad

(Prep Time: 15 min | Cooking Time: 00 min | Servings 4)

Ingredients:

- 1 rotisserie chicken, sliced
- 2 heads of romaine lettuce, shredded
- 2 cups of grape tomatoes, quartered
- 1/2 cup of mayonnaise
- ¼ cup of pine nuts
- Black pepper
- Salt

Directions:

1. Toss the lettuce with tomato, mayonnaise, pine nuts, a pinch of salt and pepper in a large mixing bowl.

2. Serve your salad with the rotisserie chicken and enjoy.

(Calories: 588 | Total Fat: 18.4 g | Protein: 85.6 g| Total Carbs: 23.6 g)

Paprika Chicken

(Prep Time: 15 min | Cooking Time: 22 min | Servings 6)

Ingredients:

- 4 pounds chicken breasts, cut into chunks
- 1 ¼ cup yellow onion, finely chopped
- 1 cup chicken broth
- 1 red bell pepper, seeded and diced
- ¼ cup coconut milk
- 1 tablespoon fresh lime juice
- 1 tablespoons coconut oil
- 2 teaspoons paprika
- 1 teaspoon red pepper flakes
- Black pepper
- Salt

Directions:

1. Season the chicken with some salt and pepper.

2. Melt the coconut oil in a large skillet, then brown chicken for 4 mins.

3. Push the chicken aside and cook the onion on the other side for 3 mins.

4. Stir in the remaining ingredients, then lower the heat and cook it for 10 to 15 mins, or until the chicken is done.

5. Serve your chicken paprika warm and enjoy.

(Calories: 643 | Total Fat: 27.5 g | Protein: 89.1 g| Total Carbs: 5.3 g)

Mediterranean Chicken Salad

(Prep Time: 15 min | Cooking Time: 35 min | Servings 4)

Ingredients:

- 2 chicken breasts
- 14 ounces artichoke heart, drained
- 1 yellow bell pepper, cut into chunks
- 1 red bell pepper, cut into chunks
- ½ cup green and black olives, halved
- 2 tablespoons lime juice
- 1 teaspoon dry oregano
- ½ teaspoon paprika
- Black pepper
- Salt

Directions:

1. Preheat the oven to 450 F.

2. Season the chicken breasts with some salt and pepper, then rub it with oregano and paprika.

3. Place the chicken breasts in a greased baking dish with the bell peppers, then cover them with a piece of foil and bake them for 35 mins.

4. Add in the olives with lime juice and artichoke hearts then serve it and enjoy.

(Calories: 508 | Total Fat: 17 g | Protein: 57.5 g| Total Carbs: 36.4 g)

Saucy Chicken Drumsticks

(Prep Time: 15 min | Cooking Time: 1 h | Servings 4)

Ingredients:

- 3 pounds chicken drumsticks

- 2 cups hot barbecue sauce

- 3 tablespoons olive oil

- 1 teaspoon onion powder

- 1 teaspoon garlic powder

- 1 teaspoon paprika

- ½ teaspoon chili powder

- 1 dash cinnamon

- Black pepper

- Salt

Directions:

1. Preheat the oven to 375 F.

2. Season the chicken drumsticks with some salt and pepper.

3. Whisk the cinnamon with paprika, olive oil, chili powder, onion and garlic powder in a small bowl, then toss it with the chicken drumsticks in a zip lock bag.

4. Lay the chicken drumsticks on a baking sheet and bake them for 25 mins, then flip

them and bake them for another 25 mins.

5. Once the time is up, broil the chicken drumsticks for 10 min.

6. Toss the chicken drumsticks with the barbecue sauce in a large bowl then serve them and enjoy.

(Calories: 860 | Total Fat: 30.4 g | Protein: 93.9 g| Total Carbs: 46.8 g)

Crust less Pepperoni Pizza

(Prep Time: 15 min | Cooking Time: 4 h 6 min | Servings 6)

Ingredients:

- 2 pounds lean sausage, crumbled
- 14 ounces pizza sauce
- 6 ounces pepperoni slices
- 2 cups cheese blend, shredded
- 2 cups mozzarella cheese, shredded
- Black pepper
- Salt

Directions:

1. Cook the sausage in a greased skillet for 6 mins, then turn off the heat and allow to cool slightly.

2. Toss the cooked sausages in a mixing bowl with the pizza sauce.

3. Mix the mozzarella cheese with the cheese blend in a bowl.

4. Place ½ of the sausage mix in the bottom of a slow cooker and top it with 1/3 of the cheese mix, then cover it with the remaining sausage.

5. Sprinkle the remaining sausage all over it, then top with the pepperoni slices.

6. Put on the lid and cook the pizza for 4 hours on low.

7. Serve your pizza warm and enjoy.

(Calories: 870 | Total Fat: 69.9 g | Protein: 49 g| Total Carbs: 8.5 g)

Bacon Chicken Sandwich

(Prep Time: 15 min | Cooking Time: 35 min | Servings 2)

Ingredients:

- 3 ounces chicken, diced
- 3 ounces cream cheese
- 2 ounces avocado, mashed
- 3 egg yolks
- 3 egg whites
- 2 grape tomato, sliced
- 2 strips bacon
- 2 slices pepper jack cheese
- 1 tablespoon of mayonnaise
- 1 teaspoon sriracha sauce
- ½ teaspoon garlic powder
- 1/8 teaspoons cream of tartar
- Black pepper
- Salt

Directions:

1. Preheat the oven to 300 F.

2. Beat the cream of tartar with egg whites and a pinch of salt until their soft peaks.

3. Beat the egg yolks with cream cheese until they become smooth and pale, then fold in the egg whites.

4. Spoon ¼ of the batter into a lined baking sheet and spread gently in the shape of a circle, then repeat the process with the remaining batter to make circles.

5. Sprinkle the garlic powder on the circles and bake them for 25 mins until they become firm to make the bread.

6. Allow the bread circles to cool down completely, then spread the mashed avocado on 2 of them.

7. Cook the bacon strips in a large skillet until they become crisp, then drain them and set them aside.

8. Season the chicken with some salt and pepper the cook it in the same skillet for 10 to 15 min or until it done.

9. Top the avocado with bacon followed by the tomato, mayonnaise, chicken, sriracha sauce and cheese.

10. Cover the sandwich with the other two bread circles, then serve them and enjoy.

(Calories: 475 | Total Fat: 36.2 g | Protein: 30.1 g| Total Carbs: 7.3 g)

Dinner

Cheese Burger Casserole

(Prep Time: 15 min | Cooking Time: 55 min | Servings 12)

Ingredients:

- 2 pounds lean beef, minced
- 1 pound bacon
- 12 ounces cheddar cheese, shredded
- 8 eggs
- 6 ounces tomato paste
- 1 cup heavy cream
- 2 cloves garlic, finely chopped
- ½ teaspoon onion powder
- Black pepper
- Salt

Directions:

1. Preheat the oven to 350 F.

2. Cook the bacon in a large skillet until it becomes crisp, then drain it and chop it.

3. Add the garlic with beef, onion powder and a pinch of salt and pepper into the same skillet with the remaining grease and cook them for 6 to 8 min.

4. Stir in the bacon, then transfer the mix into a greased baking dish.

5. Whisk the cream with eggs, tomato paste, half of the cheese and a pinch of salt and pepper in a large mixing bowl, then pour all over the beef mix.

6. Sprinkle the remaining cheese on top, then bake the burger casserole for 30 to 35 mins.

7. Once the time is up, serve it warm and enjoy.

(Calories: 548 | Total Fat: 36.3 g | Protein: 48.5 g| Total Carbs: 4.4 g)

Baked Cheesy Spaghetti

(Prep Time: 15 min | Cooking Time: 35 min | Servings 12)

Ingredients:

- 3 pounds spaghetti squash, cooked
- 3 pounds lean beef, minced
- 40 ounces marinara sauce
- 32 ounces ricotta cheese
- 30 mozzarella cheese slices
- Black pepper
- Salt

Directions:

1. Mix the beef with marinara sauce and some salt and pepper in a large bowl.

2. Place half of the spaghetti in the bottom of a greased baking dish, then top it with half of the meaty sauce, half of the mozzarella slices and ricotta cheese, then repeat the process to make a second layer with the remaining ingredients.

3. Bake the spaghetti casserole for 35 mins, then serve it warm and enjoy.

(Calories: 711 | Total Fat: 59 g | Protein: 43 g| Total Carbs: 15 g)

Caramelized Onion with Pork Chops

(Prep Time: 20 min | Cooking Time: 45 min | Servings 4)

Ingredients:

- 4 pork chops
- 6 bacon strips, sliced
- 2 small yellow onions, thinly sliced
- ½ cup chicken broth
- ¼ cup heavy cream
- Black pepper
- Salt

Directions:

1. Season the pork chops with some salt and pepper.

2. Cook the bacon in a large pan until it becomes crisp, then drain it and set it aside.

3. Add the onion to the same pan with a pinch of salt and pepper, then cook it for 15 to 20 mins, then add the bacon.

4. Brown the pork chops in the same pan for 3 mins on high on each side.

5. Lower the heat then cook the pork chops for 7 to 10 mins on each side.

6. Once the time is up, wrap the pork chops in a piece of foil and set them side.

7. Stir the cream with broth into the pan and simmer them for 3 mins to make the gravy.

8. Serve your pork chops with the bacon and onion mix and gravy and enjoy.

(Calories: 352 | Total Fat: 18.23 g | Protein: 36.98 g| Total Carbs: 6.3 g)

Bacon Avocado and Egg Salad

(Prep Time: 15 min | Cooking Time: 15 min | Servings 2)

Ingredients:

- 4 cups collard greens
- 4 eggs, boiled and peeled
- 1 ripe avocado, sliced
- 4 bacon strips, cooked and chopped
- 1 tablespoon olive oil
- Black pepper
- Salt

Directions:

1. Toss the collard greens in a large bowl with olive oil and a pinch of salt.
2. Arrange the boiled eggs with avocado and bacon, then serve your salad and enjoy.

(Calories: 569| Total Fat: 247.8 g | Protein: 25.5 g| Total Carbs: 14.7 g)

Chocolate Chili

(Prep Time: 15 min | Cooking Time: 4 h 16 min | Servings 4 to 6)

Ingredients:

- 2 pounds lean beef, minced
- 28 ounces whole canned tomato, puréed
- 8 ounces kielbasa
- 5 bacon strips, finely chopped
- 1 cup black coffee, brewed
- 1 cup beef broth
- ½ yellow onion, finely chopped
- 2 tablespoons butter
- 2 tablespoons Worcestershire sauce
- 1 tablespoon chili powder
- 1 tablespoon cocoa powder
- 1 tablespoon soy sauce
- 2 teaspoons paprika
- 2 teaspoons garlic powder
- 1 teaspoon cayenne pepper
- 1 teaspoon cumin
- Black pepper

• Salt

Directions:

1. Brown the beef in a large skillet for 6 mins, then transfer it into a slow cooker.

2. Melt the butter in the same pan and sauté ithe onion for 3 mins, then add to it the kielbasa with bacon and cook them for 6 mins.

3. Transfer the onion mix to the slow cooker with the remaining ingredients, then put on the lid and cook them for 4 hours on high.

4. Serve your chili warm and enjoy.

(Calories: 493 | Total Fat: 23.9 g | Protein: 11.5 g| Total Carbs: 56.4 g)

Fried Chicken Rice

(Prep Time: 20 min | Cooking Time: 25 min | Servings 6)

Ingredients:

- 10 ounces chicken, cooked diced
- 1 large cauliflower, diced
- 4 eggs, scrambled
- 2 bell peppers, diced
- 3 green onions, sliced
- 1 tablespoon fresh ginger, grated
- 1 tablespoon red curry paste
- ½ tablespoon coconut oil
- ½ tablespoon soy sauce
- 1 clove garlic, finely chopped
- Black pepper
- Salt

Directions:

1. Melt the coconut oil in a large pan, then sauté the onion with curry paste, ginger, bell pepper and garlic for 5 mins.

2. Add in the cauliflower and cook for 7 to 10 mins or until it is done.

3. Once the time is up, stir in the soy sauce with chicken, eggs and a pinch of salt and pepper, then cook them for 4 mins.

4. Serve your fried rice and enjoy.

(Calories: 190 | Total Fat: 6.5 g | Protein: 21.1 g| Total Carbs: 13 g)

Chicken Curry

(Prep Time: 15 min | Cooking Time: 40 min | Servings 3)

Ingredients:

- 2 chicken breasts, boneless and skinless, diced
- 2 cups chicken broth
- 1 yellow onion, thinly sliced
- 1 cups coconut milk
- 1 cup canned bamboo shoot, drained
- 3 tablespoons red curry paste
- 1 tablespoon coconut oil
- 2 cloves garlic, finely chopped
- Black pepper
- Salt

Directions:

1. Melt the coconut oil in a large pot and sauté the garlic with the onion for 3 mins, then add the chicken and cook for 6 mins.

2. Stir in the bamboo shoot with curry paste and broth, then bring them to a boil and simmer them for 20 mins.

3. Once the time is up, stir in the coconut milk with a pinch of salt and pepper, then simmer the curry for 10 mins.

4. Adjust the seasoning of the curry, then serve it with some cauliflower rice and enjoy.

(Calories: 727| Total Fat: 56.2 g | Protein: 39.9 g| Total Carbs: 18.9 g)

Caramelized Onion Pot Roast

(Prep Time: 20 min | Cooking Time: 4 h 20 min | Servings 4)

Ingredients:

- 3 pounds beef roast
- 2 white onions, sliced
- 1 ½ cup beef broth
- ½ cup balsamic vinegar
- 2 tablespoons tomato paste
- 2 tablespoons steak seasoning
- 1 tablespoon olive oil
- 4 cloves of garlic, minced
- Black pepper
- Salt

Directions:

1. Preheat the oven to 325 F.

2. Season the roast with some salt, pepper and steak seasoning.

3. Heat the oil in a large pan and brown for 3 mins on each side.

4. Lay the onion slices in the bottom of a slow cooker, then lower in it the roast.

5. Pour the broth with vinegar, garlic and tomato paste, then simmer for 5 mins, then pour them all over the roast.

6. Put on the lid and cook the roast for 4 hours on high, then serve it warm and enjoy.

(Calories: 716 | Total Fat: 25.3 g | Protein: 106.2 g| Total Carbs: 8.3 g)

Artichoke Chicken Thighs Skillet

(Prep Time: 20 min | Cooking Time: 40 min | Servings 6)

Ingredients:

- 6 large chicken thighs, skinless
- 14 ounces canned artichoke hearts, drained
- 4 cups baby spinach
- 1 cup cream cheese
- 1 cup chicken stock
- 2 cloves garlic, minced
- 1 teaspoon olive oil
- Black pepper
- Salt

Directions:

1. Preheat the oven to 400 F.

2. Heat the oil in a large skillet, then sauté the chicken with garlic for 3 mins on each side.

3. Add in the cream cheese and stir it until it melts, then add the broth and bring them to a

boil.

4. Stir in the spinach with artichoke hearts, then lower the heat and simmer for 10 mins with the lid on.

5. Once the time is up, remove the cover and bake the chicken skillet for 15 to 20 mins, then serve it warm and enjoy.

(Calories: 540 | Total Fat: 28.5 g | Protein: 60.5 g| Total Carbs: 9.2 g)

Greek Pork Chops

(Prep Time: 20 min | Cooking Time: 12 min | Servings 4)

Ingredients:

- 4 pork chops
- ¼ cup fresh lemon juice
- ¼ cup olive oil
- 2 teaspoons dry oregano
- 2 teaspoon garlic, minced
- 2 teaspoons red wine vinegar
- 1 teaspoon lemon zest, grated
- Black pepper
- Salt

Directions:

1. Season the pork chops with some salt and pepper.

2. Mix the remaining ingredients in a small bowl to make the marinade.

3. Place the pork chops in a large zip lock bag and pour the marinade all over the pork

chops, then refrigerate them for 8 hours.

    4. Preheat the grill.

    5. Grill the pork chops for 5 to 6 mins on each side

        (Calories: 373 | Total Fat: 32.7 g | Protein: 18.3 g| Total Carbs: 1.4 g)

Strawberry Chicken Salad

(Prep Time: 20 min | Cooking Time: 25 min | Servings 2)

Ingredients:

- 2 chicken breast halves
- 6 cups fresh spinach
- 8 strawberries, halved
- 1 ripe avocado, sliced
- 1 small red onion, sliced
- ¼ cup olive oil
- 1 tablespoon golden balsamic vinegar
- 1 teaspoon sugar
- Black pepper
- Salt

Directions:

1. Whisk the olive oil with vinegar, sugar and a pinch of salt in a small bowl to make the dressing.

2. Coat the chicken breasts with the dressing, then refrigerate it for 2 hours.

3. Preheat the grill and add the chicken breasts. Cook 20 to 25 mins while turning every 5 mins.

4. Toss the remaining dressing with spinach, strawberry, red onion and avocado in a large bowl, then serve them with the grilled chicken and enjoy.

(Calories: 735 | Total Fat: 50.5 g | Protein: 54.5 g| Total Carbs: 20.9 g)

Cheesy Garlic Spaghetti

(Prep Time: 15 min | Cooking Time: 10 min | Servings 2)

Ingredients:

- 1 large spaghetti squash, cooked and scraped
- 2 cups frozen spinach, finely chopped
- 1 cup mixed cheese, shredded
- 1 cup heavy cream
- ¼ cup warm water
- 2 cloves garlic, minced
- 1 cube chicken bouillon
- Black pepper
- Salt

Directions:

1. Mix the garlic in a saucepan with the chicken bouillon, cream and water. then bring them to a boil.

2. Add in the spinach and cook for 2 mins, then stir in the cheese with spaghetti and cook

them while stirring until the cheese melts.

3. Serve your spaghetti warm and enjoy.

(Calories: 587 | Total Fat: 43.6 g | Protein: 19.2 g| Total Carbs: 35.8 g)

Honey Chicken Avocado Salad

(Prep Time: 20 min | Cooking Time: 30 min | Servings 4)

Ingredients:

- 4 chicken breasts, boneless and skinless
- 4 cups romaine lettuce leaves
- 3 ripe tomatoes, sliced
- 2 cups cherry tomatos, sliced
- 1/3 cup honey
- ¼ cup bacon, diced and cooked
- 3 tablespoons whole grain mustard
- 2 tablespoons olive oil
- 2 tablespoons mild Dijon mustard
- 1 teaspoon garlic, minced
- Black pepper
- Salt

Directions:

1. Whisk the honey with olive oil, Dijon, mild mustard and garlic in a small bowl to make the marinade.

2. Season the chicken breasts with some salt and pepper, then coat with the marinade and refrigerate it for 4 hours.

3. Preheat the grill.

4. Remove the chicken from the marinade and grill for 25 to 30 mins while flipping it every 5 mins.

5. Assemble the grilled chicken with avocado, cherry tomatos, bacon and lettuce in a large serving plate, then serve it and enjoy.

(Calories: 691 | Total Fat: 33 g | Protein: 62.5 g| Total Carbs: 37.4 g)

Bell Steak Stir Fry

(Prep Time: 15 min | Cooking Time: 26 min | Servings 2)

Ingredients:

- 1 pound steak, sliced
- 1 pound asparagus, trimmed and sliced
- 1 red bell pepper, sliced
- 1 yellow onion, thinly sliced
- 1/8 cup butter
- 1 tablespoon soy sauce
- 1 tablespoon coconut oil
- 2 cloves garlic, minced
- Black pepper
- Salt

Directions:

1. Season the beef with some salt and pepper.

2. Melt the coconut oil in a large skillet, then brown the beef and garlic for 6 mins.

3. Melt the butter in another pan and sauté the onion for 5 mins, then stir in the asparagus

with the bell pepper and cook them for 6 to 10 mins or until they become tender.

4. Add the asparagus mix into the beef pan with soy sauce, then cook them for another 5 mins.

5. Serve your stir fry warm and enjoy.

(Calories: 707 | Total Fat: 30.1 g | Protein: 88.9 g| Total Carbs: 20.1 g)

Stuffed Bell Peppers

(Prep Time: 20 min | Cooking Time: 1 h | Servings 3)

Ingredients:

- 16 ounces lean beef, minced
- 3 bell peppers, seeded and halved
- 2 tomatoes, seeded and diced
- 2 cups mushrooms, sliced
- 2 cups mozzarella cheese, shredded
- ½ yellow onion, diced
- 1 tablespoon olive oil
- 1 teaspoon dry oregano
- 1 teaspoon garlic powder
- Black pepper
- Salt

Directions:

1. Preheat the oven to 350 F.

2. Heat the oil in a large skillet and sauté the onion for 2 mins, then add the beef with garlic and cook them for 10 mins.

3. Add in the oregano with the mushrooms and tomatoes and a pinch of salt and pepper, then cook them for 15 mins on low heat to make the filling.

4. Bring a pot of salted water to a boil, add the bell peppers halves and cook for 5 mins, then drain them and stuff them with the filling.

5. Sprinkle the cheese all over the stuffed bell pepper then bake them for 30 mins.

6. Once the time is up, serve them warm and enjoy.

(Calories: 673 I Total Fat: 18.1 g I Protein: 55 gI Total Carbs: 17.1 g)

Squid Spaghetti

(Prep Time: 15 min | Cooking Time: 10 min | Servings 1)

Ingredients:

- 5 ounces calamari, sliced
- 1 ounce white wine
- ½ cup tomato sauce
- 1/3 cup chicken stock
- ¼ cup parmesan cheese, grated
- ¼ cup mushrooms, sliced
- 1 tablespoon olive oil
- 1 tablespoon yellow onion, finely chopped
- ½ tablespoon basil, finely chopped
- ¼ teaspoon garlic powder
- Black pepper
- Salt

Directions:

1. Heat the oil in a large pan and sauté the garlic with onion for 1 min, then add the tomato sauce with stock and simmer them for 2 mins.

2. Stir in the white wine with mushrooms, basil, calamari and a pinch of salt and pepper, then simmer them for 5 min.

3. Once the time is up, serve your pasta warm and enjoy.

(Calories: 317 | Total Fat: 16.5 g | Protein: 24.8 g| Total Carbs: 14 g)

Nectarine Grilled Steak

(Prep Time: 15 min | Cooking Time: 20 min | Servings 2)

Ingredients:

- 8 cups baby green leaves
- 12 ounces flank steak
- ¼ cup olive oil
- 1 nectarine, sliced
- 3 tablespoons red wine vinegar
- 1 tablespoon shallots, finely chopped
- Black pepper
- Salt

Directions:

1. Preheat the grill.
2. Grill the nectarine slices for 1 min on each side.
3. Whisk the olive oil with shallots and vinegar in small bowl to make the dressing.
4. Season the steak with some salt and pepper, then rub it with half of the dressing.

5. Grill the steak for 7 to 8 mins on each side.

6. Toss the grilled nectarine with baby greens in a large bowl, then top them with the grilled steak.

7. Serve your salad and enjoy.

(Calories: 612 | Total Fat: 40.1 g | Protein: 51.6 g| Total Carbs: 12.4 g)

Garlic Parmesan Salmon Fillets

(Prep Time: 15 min | Cooking Time: 25 min | Servings 1)

Ingredients:

- 6 ounces salmon fillets
- ¼ cup parmesan cheese
- 1 tablespoon butter, melted
- 1 teaspoon mustard
- 1/8 teaspoon garlic powder
- Black pepper
- Salt

Directions:

1. Season the salmon fillet with some salt and pepper.

2. Preheat the oven to 350 F.

3. Mix the mustard with garlic powder and butter in a small bowl and spread it on the salmon fillet, then sprinkle the cheese all over it and place it on a lined baking sheet.

4. Bake the salmon fillet for 20 to 25 mins or until it is done, then serve it and enjoy.

(Calories: 435 | Total Fat: 29 g | Protein: 43.1 g| Total Carbs: 2.4 g)

Cauliflower Lasagna

(Prep Time: 20 min | Cooking Time: 40 min | Servings 8)

Ingredients:

- 1 head of cauliflower, cut into florets and steamed
- 6 ounces cream cheese
- 3 ounces pepperoni, sliced
- 3 cups mozzarella cheese
- 1 cup heavy cream
- 1 small yellow onion, diced
- 3 tablespoons tomato paste
- 2 tablespoons balsamic vinegar
- 1 tablespoon fresh basil, finely chopped
- 1 tablespoon butter
- Black pepper
- Salt

Directions:

1. Preheat the oven to 350 F.

2. Melt the butter in a large skillet and sauté onion for 3 mins, then add the garlic with vinegar and cook them for 1 min.

3. Stir in 1 cup of mozzarella cheese with tomato paste, cream cheese, heavy cream and a pinch of salt and pepper until they melt to make the sauce.

4. Simmer the sauce for 3 to 5 mins until it thickens, then stir in the basil and turn off the heat.

5. Place ½ of the steamed cauliflower in a greased baking dish and top with 1 cup of cheese and half of the pepperoni, then repeat the process to make a second layer.

6. Pour the sauce all over then bake for 20 to 25 mins.

7. Once the time is up, allow the lasagna to sit for 10 mins, then serve it warm and enjoy.

(Calories: 239 | Total Fat: 21 g | Protein: 8.4 g| Total Carbs: 5.1 g)

Cheesy Nacho Casserole

(Prep Time: 20 min | Cooking Time: 40 min | Servings 6)

Ingredients:

- 2 pounds chicken thighs, cut into bite size pieces
- 16 ounces frozen cauliflower
- 2 ounces cheddar cheese, shredded
- 2 ounces cream cheese
- 1 cup canned green chilies and tomato
- ¼ cup sour cream
- 1 jalapeno, finely chopped
- 2 tablespoons olive oil
- 1 teaspoon chili powder
- Black pepper
- Salt

Directions:

1. Preheat the oven to 375 F.
2. Season the chicken with chili powder and a pinch of salt and pepper.

3. Heat the oil in a large pan add the chicken and cook for 6 mins, then add the green chilies with tomatos and jalapeno, ¾ of the cheddar cheese, cream cheese and sour cream and keep stirring them on low heat until the cheese melts.

4. Transfer the chicken mix into a greased baking dish.

5. Microwave the cauliflower for 2 mins, then blend it smooth with the remaining cheddar cheese and a pinch of salt and pepper.

6. Spread the cauliflower mix on top, then bake it for 15 to 20 mins.

7. Once the time is up, serve your nacho casserole warm and enjoy.

(Calories: 459 | Total Fat: 24.8 g | Protein: 9.3 g| Total Carbs: 9.3 g)

Creamy Jalapeño Bacon Soup

(Prep Time: 20 min | Cooking Time: 40 min | Servings 4)

Ingredients:

- ½ pound bacon, diced
- 8 ounces cheddar cheese, shredded
- 4 jalapenos, seeded and diced
- 3 cups chicken broth
- ¾ cup heavy cream
- 4 tablespoons butter
- 1 teaspoon garlic powder
- 1 teaspoon dry thyme
- 1 teaspoon onion powder
- ½ teaspoon cumin
- Black pepper
- Salt

Directions:

1. Cook the bacon in a large skillet until it becomes crispy, then drain it and set it aside.

2. Cook the jalapenos in the same skillet for 2 mins, then drain them and set them aside.

3. Transfer the remaining bacon grease into a large pot with cumin, butter, thyme, garlic powder, onion powder and a pinch of salt and pepper, then bring them to a boil and simmer them for 15 mins on low heat.

4. Once the time is up, blend them smooth with an immersion blender, then stir in the heavy cream with cheddar cheese until they melt.

5. Stir in the bacon with jalapenos and a pinch of salt and pepper, then bring the soup to a boil and simmer it for 5 mins.

6. Serve your soup warm and enjoy.

(Calories: 476 | Total Fat: 63.6 g | Protein: 39.9 g| Total Carbs: 5.4 g)

Orange Beef Stew

(Prep Time: 15 min | Cooking Time: 5 h 10 min | Servings 4)

Ingredients:

- 2 pounds stew beef, cut into chunks
- 3 cups beef broth
- 1 yellow onion, finely chopped
- The juice of 1 orange
- 3 tablespoons coconut oil
- 2 tablespoons apple cider vinegar
- 1 tablespoon fresh thyme leaves
- 2 teaspoons cinnamon
- 2 teaspoons garlic, minced
- 1 teaspoon erythritol powder
- 1 teaspoon dry sage
- 1 teaspoon dry rosemary
- 1 teaspoon soy sauce
- Black pepper
- Salt

Directions:

1. Season the beef chunks with some salt and pepper.

2. Melt the coconut oil in a large pan and brown the beef chunks for 5 mins, then drain them and transfer them to a slow cooker.

3. Add the onion with garlic into the same pan and sauté them for 3 mins, then transfer them with the remaining ingredients to the slow cooker.

4. Put on the lid and cook the stew for 3 hours on high.

5. Once the time is up, remove the lid and cook the stew for 2 hours on high.

6. Serve your stew warm and enjoy.

(Calories: 491 | Total Fat: 25.1 g | Protein: 54.9 g| Total Carbs: 10.9 g)

Shrimp Cauliflower Curry

(Prep Time: 20 min | Cooking Time: 1 h | Servings 6)

Ingredients:

- 24 ounces of large shrimp, peeled and deveined
- 1 white onion, finely chopped
- 4 cups chicken stock
- 4 cups spinach
- 1 cup coconut milk
- ¼ cup heavy cream
- ¼ cup butter
- 3 tablespoons olive oil
- 2 tablespoons yellow curry powder
- 1 tablespoon cumin
- 2 teaspoons garlic powder
- 1 teaspoon paprika
- 1 teaspoon onion powder
- 1 teaspoon garlic powder
- 1 teaspoon chili powder
- ½ teaspoon turmeric
- Black pepper

• Salt

Directions:

1. Heat the olive oil in a large pot and sauté the onion for 3 mins, then stir in the heavy cream with butter and stir them until they melt.

2. Add the paprika with curry, onion, garlic powder, turmeric, chili powder, cumin and a pinch of salt and pepper, then cook them for 1 min.

3. Add the coconut milk and stock and bring them to a boil, then simmer them for 20 mins on low heat.

4. Once the time is up, stir in the shrimp and simmer the stew for 15 mins on low heat, uncovered.

5. Add in the spinach and simmer the stew for 5 mins, then serve it warm and enjoy.

(Calories: 549| Total Fat: 40.8 g | Protein: 36.6 g| Total Carbs: 16.3 g)

Creamy Zucchini Egg Bowl

(Prep Time: 15 min | Cooking Time: 10 h | Servings 6)

Ingredients:

- 4 pound lamb leg
- ½ cup olive oil
- 4 tablespoons whole grain mustard
- 2 tablespoons maple syrup
- 4 sprigs fresh thyme
- 1 ½ teaspoon garlic powder
- 1 ½ teaspoon dry rosemary
- Black pepper
- Salt

Directions:

1. Whisk the fresh thyme with olive oil, mustard, maple syrup, rosemary and garlic powder in a small bowl to make the marinade.

2. Season the lamb leg with some salt and pepper, then place it in a large slow cooker and coat it with the marinade.

3. Put on the lid and cook it for 10 hours on low.

4. Once the time is up, drain the lamb leg and place it on a lined baking sheet, then roast it in the preheated oven for 15 mins.

5. Serve your lamb leg warm and enjoy.

(Calories: 734 | Total Fat: 39.4 g | Protein: 85 g| Total Carbs: 5.8 g)

Thai Peanut Chicken

(Prep Time: 15 min | Cooking Time: 20 min | Servings 6)

Ingredients:

- 2 pounds of chicken thighs, cut into bite size pieces
- ½ cup peanut butter
- ¼ cup chicken broth
- 2 tablespoons soy sauce
- 1 tablespoon orange juice
- 1 tablespoon lemon juice
- ½ tablespoon coconut oil
- 2 teaspoons chili garlic sauce
- ¼ teaspoon cayenne pepper
- Black pepper
- Salt

Directions:

1. Season the chicken with some salt and pepper.

2. Melt the coconut oil in a large pan, then sauté the chicken for 8 mins.

3. Combine the peanut butter with stock, garlic sauce, lemon and orange juice, soy sauce, cayenne pepper and a pinch of salt and pepper in a blender, then blend them smooth to make the sauce.

4. Pour the sauce all over the chicken, then simmer it for 10 mins.

5. Serve your Thai peanut chicken warm with some cauliflower rice and enjoy.

(Calories: 430 | Total Fat: 23.2 g | Protein: 49.7 g| Total Carbs: 5.1 g)

Dessert

Cheesecake Pumpkin Mousse

(Prep Time: 15 min | Cooking Time: 00 min | Servings 12)

Ingredients:

- 16 ounces cream cheese
- 15 ounces pumpkin purée
- 2 cups heavy cream
- 2 teaspoons pumpkin spice
- 1 teaspoon liquid Stevia
- 1 teaspoon vanilla extract

Directions:

1. Combine the pumpkin purée with cream cheese in a stand mixer and mix them until they become smooth.

2. Add in the remaining ingredients and whip them for 5 mins.

3. Once the time is up, pipe the mousse into serving cups, then serve it and enjoy.

(Calories: 214 | Total Fat: 21 g | Protein: 3.9 g| Total Carbs: 4.2 g)

Pumpkin Butter Coffee

(Prep Time: 10 min | Cooking Time: 00 min | Servings 1)

Ingredients:

- 12 ounces hot brewed coffee
- 2 tablespoons pumpkin purée
- 1 tablespoon butter
- ¼ teaspoon pumpkin spice
- Liquid Stevia to taste

Directions:

1. Combine all the ingredients in a food processor and blend them smooth.
2. Serve your coffee right away and enjoy.

(Calories: 120 | Total Fat: 12 g | Protein: 1 g| Total Carbs: 3 g)

Chocolate Pie

(Prep Time: 15 min | Cooking Time: 12 min | Servings 4)

Ingredients:

- 2 cups almond flour
- 2 cups heavy cream
- ¼ cup of cocoa powder
- 3 egg whites
- 3 tablespoons butter, melted
- 3 teaspoons Splenda
- 1 teaspoons chilled coffee
- 1/8 teaspoon liquid Stevia
- Salt

Directions:

1. Preheat the oven to 350 F.

2. Mix the butter with almond flour, ¼ cup cocoa powder, 1 teaspoon of Splenda, Stevia and a pinch of salt in a mixing bowl, then mix them until they become smooth.

3. Spoon the mix into a baking pan to make the crust and bake it for 12 mins, then set it aside to cool down.

4. Beat the egg whites with 2/3 cup of cocoa powder, 2 teaspoons of Splenda, coffee, heavy cream and a pinch of salt in a large bowl until they become fluffy and light to make the filling.

5. Pour the filling into the crust, bake it then chill it in the fridge for 2 hours then serve it and enjoy.

(Calories: 630 | Total Fat: 57.2 g | Protein: 17.6 g| Total Carbs: 26 g)

Chocolate Mousse

(Prep Time: 15 min | Cooking Time: 00 min | Servings 4)

Ingredients:

- 8,5 ounces mascarpone cheese
- 2 tablespoons cocoa powder, unsweetened
- 1 tablespoon of a sweetener
- 1 teaspoon vanilla extract

Directions:

1. Combine all the ingredients in a large bowl and whip them until they become fluffy.
2. Spoon the mousse into serving cups, then serve them and enjoy.

(Calories: 286 | Total Fat: 27 g | Protein: 4 g| Total Carbs: 2 g)

Pomegranate Pudding

(Prep Time: 15 min | Cooking Time: 10 min | Servings 4)

Ingredients:

- 14.5 ounces coconut milk
- ½ cup pomegranate seeds
- 3 tablespoons raw honey
- 2 tablespoons coconut oil
- 1 tablespoon vanilla extract
- 1 packet gelatin, unflavored

Directions:

1. Melt the coconut oil in a large saucepan, then stir in the honey with coconut milk and vanilla extract.

2. Cook the coconut mix until it starts bubbling, then stir in the gelatin gently until it completely melts.

3. Stir in the pomegranate seeds and pour the mix into serving cups, then refrigerate them for 4 hours.

4. Serve the coconut pudding and enjoy.

(Calories: 386 | Total Fat: 31.3 g | Protein: 8.6 g| Total Carbs: 21.5 g)

Berry Lemon Cake

(Prep Time: 15 min | Cooking Time: 30 min | Servings 6)

Ingredients:

- ½ cup fresh blueberries
- ½ cup coconut flour
- 1/3 cup coconut milk
- 1/3 cup raw honey
- 3 eggs, beaten
- 2 ½ tablespoons coconut oil, melted
- 2 tablespoons fresh lemon juice
- 1 tablespoon lemon zest, grated
- 1 teaspoon lemon extract
- 1 teaspoon apple cider vinegar
- ½ teaspoon baking soda
- Salt

Directions:

1. Preheat the oven to 350 F.

2. Mix the apple cider with baking soda in a small bowl.

3. Mix the baking soda mix with coconut oil, lemon juice and zest, lemon extract, coconut flour and honey, coconut milk, eggs and a pinch of salt until no lumps are found, then fold in the berries.

4. Pour the batter into a greased baking dish, then bake it for 30 mins.

5. Once the time is up, allow the cake to cool down for 10 mins, then serve and enjoy.

(Calories: 203 | Total Fat: 13.4 g | Protein: 3.5 g| Total Carbs: 19.6 g)

Vanilla Cupcakes

(Prep Time: 15 min | Cooking Time: 30 min | Servings 32)

Ingredients:

- 1 cup almond milk, unsweetened
- 1 cup almond flour
- ¾ cup erythritol, powdered
- ½ cup butter
- 7 eggs
- 1 tablespoon baking powder
- 3 teaspoons vanilla extract
- ½ teaspoon liquid stevia
- Salt

Directions:

1. Preheat the oven to 350 F.
2. Combine all the ingredients in a large bowl and mix them until no lumps are found.
3. Pour the batter into cupcake liners, then bake them for 28 to 30 mins.
4. Allow the cupcakes to cool, then serve them with your favorite toppings and enjoy.

(Calories: 100 | Total Fat: 7.1 g | Protein: 2.1 g| Total Carbs: 8 g)

Cocoa Mocha Truffles

(Prep Time: 15 min | Cooking Time: 00 min | Servings 15 to 20)

Ingredients:

- 7 ounces butter, unsalted
- 4 tablespoons strong brewed coffee
- 2 tablespoons honey
- 2 tablespoons cocoa powder
- ½ teaspoon vanilla powder
- ½ teaspoon cinnamon
- Salt

Directions:

1. Combine all the ingredients, with a pinch of salt, in a mixing bowl and mix them until they become smooth.

2. Spoon 2 teaspoons of the mix and shape it into balls, then roll them in some cocoa powder or chopped nuts.

3. Repeat the process with the remaining mix, freeze them for 1 hour, then serve them and enjoy.

(Calories: 93| Total Fat: 9.6 g | Protein: 0.2 g| Total Carbs: 2.5 g)

Vanilla Ice Cream

(Prep Time: 20 min | Cooking Time: 00 min | Servings 6)

Ingredients:

- 4 egg whites
- 4 egg yolks
- 1 ¼ cup heavy whipping cream
- ½ cup erythritol, powdered
- 1 tablespoon vanilla extract
- ¼ teaspoon cream of tartar

Directions:

1. Beat the egg whites with cream of tartar in a large bowl until they're soft peaks while adding the powdered erythritol.

2. Whisk the whipped cream in another bowl until it's soft peaks.

3. Whisk the egg yolks until they become pale, then add the vanilla and whisk them again.

4. Fold the whipped cream into the egg whites, then add the egg yolks and fold them gently.

5. Spoon the mix into a loaf pan and freeze it for 2 hours, then serve your ice cream and enjoy.

(Calories: 226 | Total Fat: 12.3 g | Protein: 4.8 g| Total Carbs: 24.9 g)

Peanut Butter Chocolate Cake

(Prep Time: 10 min | Cooking Time: 1 min | Servings 1)

Ingredients:

- 2 tablespoons erythritol powder
- 2 tablespoons cocoa powder, unsweetened
- 1 egg
- 1 tablespoon heavy whipping cream
- 1 tablespoons peanut butter
- ½ teaspoon vanilla extract
- ¼ teaspoon baking powder
- Salt

Directions:

1. Whisk all the ingredients in a mixing bowl until no lumps are found.
2. Pour the batter into a greased ramekin and microwave it for 1 min.
3. Serve your cake and enjoy.

(Calories: 226 | Total Fat: 3.2 g | Protein: 2 g| Total Carbs: 1.8 g)

Snow Bites

(Prep Time: 20 min | Cooking Time: 18 min | Servings 36)

Ingredients:

- 2 cups almond flour
- 1 cup walnuts, finely chopped
- ¾ and ½ cup erythritol, powdered
- ½ cup butter, softened
- 1 egg
- 2 tablespoons coconut flour
- 1 teaspoon vanilla extract
- 1 teaspoon baking powder
- ¾ teaspoon cardamom powder
- ¼ teaspoon Stevia extract
- Salt

Directions:

1. Preheat the oven to 325 F.

2. Mix the cardamom powder with a pinch of salt, coconut flour, walnut, baking powder and almond flour in a mixing bowl.

3. Beat ½ cup of erythritol with butter in a mixing bowl until it becomes light and fluffy, then add the egg with Stevia and vanilla and beat them again.

4. Add the almond mix to the butter and mix them until they make smooth dough, then shape it into ¾ inch balls.

5. Place the dough balls on 2 lined baking sheets and bake them for 18 mins.

6. Once the time is up, toss the almond balls in a large bowl gently with ¾ cup of erythritol until coated, then serve them and enjoy.

(Calories: 40 | Total Fat: 7.4 g | Protein: 2.1 g| Total Carbs: 5.5 g)

Blueberry Ice Cream

(Prep Time: 15 min | Cooking Time: 00 min | Servings 4)

Ingredients:

- 1 cup heavy whipping cream
- ½ cup crème fraiche
- ½ cup blueberries
- 2 egg yolks
- 1 tablespoon vanilla powder

Directions:

1. Whip the whipping cream until it becomes fluffy, then set it aside.

2. Beat the crème fraiche until it becomes fluffy, then add the whipping cream, vanilla, blueberries and egg yolks and beat them again until they become creamy.

3. Spoon the ice cream into a loaf pan and freeze it for 1 hour then serve it and enjoy.

(Calories: 202 | Total Fat: 19 g | Protein: 2.4 g| Total Carbs: 4.6 g)

Pecan Pie Ice Cream

(Prep Time: 15 min | Cooking Time: 00 min | Servings 4)

Ingredients:

- 2 cups coconut milk
- ½ cup pumpkin purée
- ½ cup cottage cheese
- ½ cup pecans, toasted and chopped
- 1/3 cup erythritol, powdcrcd
- 3 egg yolks
- 20 drops liquid Stevia
- 1 teaspoon pumpkin spice
- 1 teaspoon maple extract
- ½ teaspoon xantham gum powder

Directions:

1. Combine all the ingredients in a large container (except for the pecans) and blend them with an immersion blender until they become smooth.

2. Pour the mix into an ice cream machine and stir in the toasted pecans, then prepare it according to the manufacturer's instructions.

3. Serve your ice cream and enjoy.

(Calories: 467 | Total Fat: 37.2 g | Protein: 6 g| Total Carbs: 34.3 g)

Chocolate Bites

(Prep Time: 20 min | Cooking Time: 20 min | Servings 20)

Ingredients:

- 1 cup almond flour
- 1/3 cup coconut, shredded
- 1/3 cup erythritol, powdered
- ¼ cup coconut oil
- ¼ cup cocoa powder
- 2 eggs
- 3 tablespoons coconut flour
- 1 teaspoon vanilla extract
- ½ teaspoon baking powder
- Salt

Directions:

1. Preheat the oven to 350 F.

2. Mix the shredded coconut and coconut flour with cocoa powder, erythritol, almond flour, baking powder and a pinch of salt in a large bowl.

3. Add the vanilla with coconut oil and eggs, then knead them to get smooth dough.

4. Shape the dough into 20 balls, then place them on a lined baking sheet and bake them for 15 to 20 mins.

5. Once the time is up, serve your chocolate bites and enjoy.

(Calories: 85 | Total Fat: 6.4 g | Protein: 1.9 g| Total Carbs: 6.7 g)

Swiss Roll

(Prep Time: 25 min | Cooking Time: 15 min | Servings 12)

Ingredients:

- 8 ounces cream cheese
- 1 cup almond flour
- ½ cup erythritol, powder
- ½ cup sour cream
- ¼ cup cocoa powder
- ¼ cup coconut milk
- ¼ cup psyllium husk powder
- 12 tablespoons butter
- 3 eggs
- 2 teaspoons vanilla extract
- 1 teaspoon baking powder
- ¼ teaspoon liquid Stevia
- Salt

Directions:

1. Mix the almond flour with ¼ cup of cocoa powder, psyllium husk powder, baking powder, ¼ cup of erythritol and a pinch of salt in a large mixing bowl.

2. Add in 4 tablespoons of butter with coconut milk, ¼ cup of sour cream, eggs and 1 tea-

spoon of vanilla extract and mix them again until they become smooth.

3. Preheat the oven to 350 F.

4. Transfer the mix to a lined baking sheet and press it to make the crust, then bake it for 12 to 15 mins.

5. Beat the remaining 8 tablespoons of butter with ¼ cup of erythritol, 1 teaspoon of vanilla, Stevia, ¼ cup of sour cream and cream cheese until they become light and fluffy to make the filling.

6. Spread the filling all over the crust and roll it gently.

7. Serve your Swiss Roll with your favorite toppings and enjoy.

(Calories: 274.2 | Total Fat: 25.1 g | Protein: 5.3 g| Total Carbs: 6.8 g)

Keto Brownies

(Prep Time: 15 min | Cooking Time: 20 min | Servings 8)

Ingredients:

- 2 cups almond flour
- ½ cup cocoa powder
- 1/3 cup erythritol, powdered
- ¼ cup maple syrup
- ¼ cup coconut oil
- 2 eggs
- 2 tablespoons keto caramel
- 1 tablespoon psyllium husk powder
- 1 teaspoon baking powder
- Salt

Directions:

1. Preheat the oven to 350 F.

2. Mix all the ingredients in a large mixing bowl with a pinch of salt until you get smooth dough.

3. Press the mix into a greased baking pan and bake it for 20 mins.

4. Once the time is up, allow the brownies to cool completely, then serve them and enjoy.

(Calories: 258.1 | Total Fat: 23.7 g | Protein: 8 g| Total Carbs: 10.4 g)

Lime Cake

(Prep Time: 25 min | Cooking Time: 40 min | Servings 10)

Ingredients:

- 1 cup almond flour
- 5 egg whites
- 5 egg yolks
- ¼ cup erythritol, powdered
- ¼ cup cream cheese
- ¼ cup blueberries
- 2 tablespoons butter
- The juice of 1 lime
- 2 tablespoons coconut flour
- 2 teaspoons blueberry extract
- 1 teaspoon baking powder
- ¼ teaspoon liquid Stevia
- Salt

Directions:

1. Preheat the oven to 325 F.

2. Mix the almond flour with coconut flour, baking powder and a pinch of salt in a large mixing bowl.

3. Beat the egg yolks until they become pale, then add the blueberry extract, butter, cream cheese, ¼ cup of erythritol and Stevia, then beat them again until they become smooth.

4. Add the lime juice, beat them again, then fold in the flour mix until no lumps are found.

5. Beat the egg whites in a large bowl until they're soft peaks, then fold in the egg yolk batter.

6. Fold in the blueberries and pour the batter into two small greased loaf pans, then bake them for 35 to 40 mins.

7. Once the time is up, serve your cake and enjoy.

(Calories: 164 | Total Fat: 11.4 g | Protein: 5.7 g| Total Carbs: 11 g)

Chocolate Chip Cookies

(Prep Time: 25 min | Cooking Time: 15 min | Servings 16)

Ingredients:

- 1 cup almond flour
- ½ cup keto chocolate chips
- 8 tablespoons butter
- ¼ cup erythritol, powdered
- 3 tablespoons whey protein
- 2 tablespoons coconut flour
- 2 tablespoons psyllium husk powder
- 1 egg
- 2 teaspoons vanilla extract
- 10 drops liquid Stevia
- ½ teaspoon baking powder
- Salt

Directions:

1. Preheat the oven to 350 F.

2. Beat the butter with erythritol in a large mixing bowl until they become light and

fluffy, then add the vanilla and egg and beat them again.

3. Add in the remaining ingredients (except for the chocolate) then mix them until no lumps are found.

4. Fold in the chocolate chips, then shape the dough into 16 balls and press them slightly.

5. Place the dough balls on a lined baking sheet and bake them for 12 to 15 mins, then serve them and enjoy.

(Calories: 155 | Total Fat: 10.9 g | Protein: 3.5 g| Total Carbs: 13.5 g)

Italian Spongy Lemon Cake

(Prep Time: 20 min | Cooking Time: 25 min | Servings 8)

Ingredients:

- 1 cup almond flour
- 5 egg yolks
- 5 egg whites
- ¼ cup erythritol, powdered
- 2 tablespoons olive oil
- 1 teaspoon almond extract
- 1 teaspoon vanilla extract
- 1 teaspoon baking powder
- The zest of half a lemon, grated
- ½ teaspoon cream of tartar
- ¼ teaspoon of liquid Stevia
- Salt

Directions:

1. Preheat the oven to 325 F.

2. Mix the vanilla with almond extract and egg yolk in a mixing bowl until they become pale then add to the erythritol with almond flour, baking powder, lemon zest and a pinch of salt and mix them again.

3. Whip the egg whites with cream of tartar until they're soft peaks, then fold in the egg yolk mix.

4. Pour the batter into a greased baking pan and bake it for 25 mins.

5. Once the time is up, serve your cake with your favorite toppings and enjoy.

(Calories: 180 | Total Fat: 12.3 g | Protein: 6.5 g| Total Carbs: 12.4 g)

Allspice Chocolate Soufflé

(Prep Time: 20 min | Cooking Time: 1 h | Servings 4)

Ingredients:

- 1 cup coconut milk
- 1 cup keto scones leftovers, crumbled
- 2 eggs yolks
- 2 egg whites
- 2 tablespoons butter
- 1 teaspoon allspice

Directions:

1. Preheat the oven to 400 F.

2. Microwave the coconut milk for 1 min, then stir in the scones leftovers and set them aside.

3. Beat the egg whites until they're soft peaks.

4. Whisk the allspice with butter and egg yolks in a mixing bowl until they become smooth, then stir in the scones mix.

5. Fold in the egg whites, then spoon the batter into 4 greased ramekins.

6. Bake the soufflés for 40 to 50 mins, then serve them and enjoy.

(Calories: 445.5 | Total Fat: 39.8 g | Protein: 8 g| Total Carbs: 12.5 g)

Conclusion

Thank you again for downloading this book! I really do hope you found the recipes as tasty and mouthwatering as I did!

About The Author

Professional dietitian and fitness expert, Teresa McCaine, was born in 1969 in the United states and resides there with her family. She is a nutritional scientist with over 15 years of professional experience. Raised in a unique and small family, the practice of healthy eating has been one strictly followed by her family and has since remain a part of her life. She is a graduate of the University of Illinois, Chicago, US, with BS in nutrition and currently works as a professional nutritionist.

She enhanced her education by studying and practicing at the West Chester University, Pennsylvania and also gained extensive clinical experience and taught food nutrition at college level in New Zealand.

Passionate about working with people with food intolerances, she serves her clients by conducting in-depth consultations by providing individually tailored recommendation regarding lifestyle, nutrition, herbal medicine, yoga, and general body fitness. Knowing the link between food intolerance and chronic conditions, such as rheumatoid arthritis, diabetes, and cancer has been Teresa's focal point in research as well as clinical practices.

She has gain popularity for herself in her community as she is known as a mentor, educator, advisor, author and mother. Her professional experience coupled with the live-changing experience she encountered with the numerous clients she faced, made it possible for her to have written this book "30 Days Keto Neal plan" Get rid of The Extra Weight with 120 keto recipes in a bid to helps different individuals and family keep a good shape, eat good, and live a healthy lifestyle.

Teresa is friendly and has a loving personality. She likes spending time with her friends and family and enjoys practicing yoga with her daughter. She is enthusiast about learning and researching healthy lifestyles for friends and family. She loves practicing what she preaches and stand by her values of living a healthy non-toxic lifestyle.

91691830R00119

Made in the USA
Lexington, KY
24 June 2018